AF673913

POLITICAL BEHAVIOUR

Political Behaviour

Edited by

Dipali Saha

GLOBAL VISION PUBLISHING HOUSE
20, Ansari Road, Daryaganj, New Delhi-110002 (INDIA)

GLOBAL VISION PUBLISHING HOUSE
F-4, 1st Floor, 'Hari Sadan'
20, Ansari Road, Daryaganj, New Delhi-110002 (INDIA)
Tel.: 30971125, 23261581 Mob: 9810644769
Email: nsingh_2004@vsnl.net; Website: globalvisionpub.com

Political Behaviour

© Editor

First Edition, 2005

ISBN: 81-8220-097-0

[Responsibility for the facts stated, opinions expressed, conclusions reached and plagiarism, if any, in this title is entirely that of the Contributors. The Editor and Publisher bear no responsibility for them whatsoever. All rights reserved. No part of this book may be reproduced in any manner without written permission.]

PRINTED IN INDIA

Published by Dr. N.K. Singh for Global Vision Publishing House, New Delhi-2 and *Printed at* Balaji Offset, Naveen Shahdara, Delhi-32.

Preface

It is useful to begin this study with the many references to institutional support for political behaviour in order to make the point that there were many new, highly relevant and organisational initiatives outside the halls of the academy proper. In their newness, the leaders of the initiatives conveyed a shared sense of optimism and challenge that encouraged members of the political science research community to explore new work ways. The study of political behaviour was first introduced in 1952 with the first US national election study that was carried out by the Political Behaviour Programme of the University of Michigan's Survey Research Center.

As a consequence, new research is less often inspired by the prospect of a new venture into heretofore unchartered domains of politics and government and more often a trek through essentially familiar terrain in a new analytic vehicle. The evolution of new analytic perspectives and techniques has, of course, been made possible largely through the agency of the computer, a second source of transformations from the old to the new. There will certainly be an extra-ordinary increase in the sheer volume of research. Technical standards will almost certainly go up on all fronts—data collection, data analysis and theoretical explanations of political behaviour in varied settings.

It seems to me that we are not in the process of developing a new model of the democratic citizen so much as we are learning about the conditions and circumstances under which varied and different categories of citizens respond politically in understandably different ways. Although much political philosophy and much élite political behaviour rests on one or another conception of the average or typical or modal member of the rank and file citizenry. Much of the research on large populations, such as national electorates, documents the heterogeneity of responses to common stimuli.

What we have learnt from this study about mass electoral behaviour certainly has meaning for the theories of democratic politics. But as yet we are often uncertain as to what the various meanings ultimately will be. It may be that greater self-conscious attention to the assumptions that underlie democratic theory would channel programmes of research to meet various challenges posed by the theory. Thus far the meandering course of research into mass electoral behaviour has more often followed the decisions of scholars intent on better 'understanding' some obvious feature of political topography than testing a normative construction.

Contents

1
Introduction

The fiftieth anniversy of the modern era in political behaviour research was celebrated (quite silently) in 1994. We mark 1944 as the birth of the modern era because in that year Paul Lazarsfeld and his colleagues from the Bureau of Applied Social Research at Columbia University published the first academically inspired study of an election that focused primarily on individual voters. Their study, which reported on fieldwork carried out in the 1940 presidential campaign in Elmira, New York, was quite primitive in some respects and quite advanced in others. Moreover, it established an enduring intellectual paradigm in political behaviour research—an intellectual paradigm that we will consider more extensively below. But the fundamental significance of their study for the modern era was that it focused on individual voters, and in so doing it helped transform the study of citizenship and democratic politics.

The Columbia sociologists were not the only scholars during this general period who turned their focus to the individual citizen. Two other streams of intellectual research, both of which understood democratic politics in the context of individual voters, locate their origins in the same postwar period. The American National Election Study series and the work of Campbell, Converse,

Miller and Stokes trace their origins to fieldwork conducted in the 1948 election.[1] And economic theories of democracy have a genesis which dates, perhaps most notably, to the work of Anthony Downs.[2] Taken together, these efforts have established three schools of research: the political sociology tradition that flowed from the work of the Bureau of Applied Research at Columbia, the political psychology tradition with origins at the University of Michigan's Center for Survey Research, and the political economy tradition which seriously began to apply concepts of rationality and self-interest to the study of citizen behaviour.

The danger in identifying these separate traditions is that we ignore their commonalities to focus on their differences, thereby missing the forest for the trees. The thesis of this chapter is that each of the three traditions addressed a distinct challenge to democratic theory. Each tradition has made substantial progress in formulating a response to these distinctive challenges, but in moving toward a response, they have also tended to converge on a unified view of the citizen in democratic politics. We might indeed say that the convergence has produced a new empirical model of the democratic citizen, and hence an updated vision of democratic politics. None of this is meant to suggest that important differences do not continue to exist—much of this chapter will be devoted to an examination of their implications. We do intend to point out the revolution that the three traditions commonly fostered in the study of electoral politics, the common intellectual problems that they addressed, and the convergence that has marked their development through time.

Where do the commonalities originate? Most important, all these studies share a common focus on individual voters—a focus that is enduring in political behaviour research. Moreover, each in a different way called into question the capacity of individual citizens to function in democratic politics, thereby presenting a challenge to democratic theory. Indeed, it is no exaggeration to say that this challenge has supplied much of the intellectual agenda for political behaviour research during the past 50 years. Political sociologists have been forced to confront social determinism as a challenge to the model of the independent citizen. Political psychologists have confronted the political knowledge vacuum that characterises typical citizens, and the implications that arise for theories of democracy that depend on astute and politically sophisticated citizen decision-makers. Political economists have posed perhaps the ultimate riddle of citizenship: why would a rational individual invest in the duties of citizenship when the effect of each individual investment is likely to be trivial and unimportant?

At the same time that each tradition has addressed a distinctive challenge to the capacity of individual citizens and hence to the potential of democratic politics, all the three have produced a high degree of convergence in their responses. Each tradition has arrived at a reconciliation, of sorts, between the capacities of flesh-and-blood citizens and the theoretical requirements imposed by democratic politics. But in arriving at the reconciliation, a new empirical model of citizenship has evolved which, in many respects, is common across the three traditions. And the point of convergence among the three traditions is the purposeful, instrumentally motivated citizen.

The purposeful, instrumentally motivated citizen is, of course, the citizen embodied in political economy traditions. Thus, in a crucial sense, it was this model of citizenship and this tradition of scholarship that posed the fundamental challenge to political behaviour research. In other words, the political economy tradition encouraged both the political sociology and political psychology traditions to reconsider—and in the process, rediscover—their own roots in the analysis of purposeful citizens and political behaviour.

The Economic Interpretation

We begin this chapter by considering briefly the challenge to traditional views of democratic citizenship posed by the political economy tradition. We then show that, somewhat ironically, in spite of the dead end to which the model of democratic citizenship ultimately led, it fostered a revival of interest in the study of purposeful, instrumentally motivated citizenship in political behaviour research more generally: Our purpose is not to review the entire field of political behaviour research but instead to identify emergent streams in this research that exemplify this renewed view of democratic citizenship.

Perhaps the most fundamental challenge to traditional visions of democratic citizenship was posed by Anthony Downs in his articulation of an "economic theory of democracy."[3] If citizens act rationally on the basis of individually defined self-interest, Downs showed, they might very well abstain from voting in elections. Rational abstention is a quite sensible response when the benefits that any voter obtains due to participation are compared to the costs of participation, after these benefits are discounted by the microscopically small likelihood that any single voter will play a pivotal role in an election outcome. Indeed, based on such a calculus, it becomes quite clear that the only reasonable course of action is to refrain from voting.

The same calculation can be invoked in the analysis of other citizenship activities as well. Most particularly, the costs of becoming informed about politics are often much higher than the costs of voting, and hence the same underlying analysis comes into play. Citizens might act more strategically to realize their interests if they based their actions on better, more complete information. But given the minimal likelihood that any single act will be pivotal, what is the use? Why should anyone bother to become informed?

Downs's analysis of rational abstention and the costs of becoming informed foreshadowed a more general scholarly assault on a wide range of collective action problems more broadly conceived, most particularly Olson's analysis of political organisation and the challenge of securing a membership.[4] Perhaps the ultimate tribute to both analyses is that they have stimulated so much intellectual activity, both within and beyond the political economy tradition. A significant portion of this intellectual effort has been aimed at a reconciliation between the expectations that are generated by the political economy models and the empirical reality as we know it. That is, given the strong individually based incentives for free-riding and shirking responsibility, why does *anyone* participate in elections, join organisations, or stay informed about politics? Perhaps ironically, the task of reconciling theoretical expectations with empirical reality is more readily accomplished with respect to political organisation. The importance of coercion, selective incentives, and institutional arrangements[5] for the long-term maintenance and survival of political co-operation is now widely accepted, *albeit* with some dissenters.[6]

The more difficult challenge has arisen with respect to the most widespread and basic citizenship duties—the decision to participate in elections and stay informed about politics. At the same time that Downs makes a persuasive case for rational abstention—and more than a few political scientists have been converted to personal non-participation as a result!—we witness the riddle of relatively widespread participation. Moreover, and particularly in the American case, levels of information and participation are highest among the best educated—those who should be best able to understand and comprehend that the exercise of citizenship duties is not in their own individual best interests. In short, the simple and persuasive logic of rational abstention runs opposite to some straightforward empirical evidence with respect to the functioning of democratic politics.

Rational Citizenship

A great deal of ink has been spilled in the effort to resolve this riddle. Beginning in the 1960s, political economists began an effort to reconcile the facts of widespread participation with the logic of rational abstention—an effort that was perhaps made more urgent by a chorus of critics who viewed the idea of rational citizenship as a crackpot idea. We do not possess the inclination, and this is not the place, to engage in an extensive review of these efforts, except to say that they have mostly failed.[7] Finally and fundamentally, widespread information-seeking and voting in elections cannot be understood from the vantage-point of short-term rational calculation because, as Fiorina argues, participation and the acquisition of information are activities that are valued intrinsically.[8] People perform citizenship duties because they like to, or because they feel guilty if they don't, or because it is embarrassing to look stupid during lunch-time conversation. The important point is that the performance of citizenship duties takes on value as an end in itself.

Does this mean that voters are not rational? Or more importantly, does it mean that we cannot profitably view the decision to become informed and vote within the context of a rational calculus? These are fairly absurd questions, and their absurdity might be highlighted by analogy with an example of pure (rational) consumer behaviour. One of the authors drives a Volvo while the other drives General Motors products. The GM buyer believes that his Volvo co-author has perverse preferences that lead to the expenditure of a great deal of money that might be used more productively elsewhere—at least more productively with respect to the GM buyer's preferences. But the co-author likes Volvos. He might even be willing to make an argument that Volvos are worth the additional expense, but finally he just likes Volvos. Now if the exchange rate changed and the price of Volvos went even higher, the co-author might get smart and buy a Chevrolet. And hence, the Volvo co-author is not irrational. He just likes Volvos.

By demonstrating that rational abstention is the best solution for citizens who base their decision to vote on narrowly defined self-interest, Downs showed us that widespread participation is best understood as a manifestation of an activity that is valued intrinsically. Citizens who read the *New York Times* and vote are not irrational—they just like to vote, or maybe they feel bad when they don't vote. Their preferences are not determinate, however. If the election campaign is particularly nasty, or if the candidates are both unattractive, or if the outcome is a foregone conclusion, or if there is a blizzard on election day, they may stay home. In short, their preference for voting is not absolute, it is simply one of the factors they take into account when deciding whether to vote.

Unfortunately, the discussion of rational citizenship took an unproductive turn that led down a blind alley. Arguments regarding whether citizens are rational tend to be very unproductive affairs. One measure of the success realised by the political economy tradition is the extent to which it has encouraged other traditions of political behaviour to rediscover their own roots in the analysis of purposeful citizens and political behaviour. Much of the development of these traditions must be seen against the backdrop of the rediscovery of purposeful citizenship by political scientists.

Indeed, much of the progress in political behaviour research during the past forty years, beginning with Simon's work, has come in response to the political economist's challenge—the challenge to rediscover the role of purposeful citizens in the workings of democratic politics.[9] We are not suggesting that game theory has or should become the vocabulary of choice among political scientists, or that other traditions in political behaviour research have been submerged in a rational choice paradigm. Quite to the contrary, we argue that the other traditions in political behaviour research have relocated the role of purposeful citizens in their own unfolding intellectual histories.

Sociological Responses to Political Behaviour

A central insight of the Columbia school was that social attributes are important not because they translate directly and deterministically to a set of interests and concomitant preferences, but rather because they locate individuals in social structure and hence affect exposure to political information.[10] While this is a sophisticated argument with powerful consequences, the early Columbia work, and in particular *The People's Choice*, provided its critics with a ready target. Consider the following formulation of the authors' argument:

> "a person thinks, politically, as he is, socially. Social characteristics determine political preference".[11]

Framed in this way, and perhaps taken out of context, it may be difficult to imagine a more straightforward statement of social determinism. Where did such a statement of the problem leave political science? Was politics simply a residue of social life? Was political science best seen as a subfield within sociology? In their classic response, Key and Munger seek to establish the unique, independent, and idiosyncratic character of politics.[12] Based on political histories within Indiana counties, they argue that the development of political loyalties takes peculiar and unexpected turns, and hence there is no simple one-to-one correspondence between political preference and social characteristics. Political preferences are connected to social characteristics in one way at one place, but in quite another way at another place. Hence, politics is not a simple residue of social life, and political preference is not simply and socially determined.

The Key and Munger response is often cited as a refutation of the social determinism thought to be inherent in the Columbia studies, but more importantly it provides a political scientist's reconstruction of the political sociological tradition. The Key and Munger argument is a direct assault on the idea that political preference is the direct consequence of political interest defined in terms of individual characteristics. If we want to understand Indiana voters, the inference becomes, we must understand them where they reside, in the circumstances that surround them, and such an under-taking cannot be accomplished if we study them simply as individuals who are divorced from a place and time.

Key's contribution to the political sociological tradition is perhaps best understood with respect to his analysis of white voters in the context of *Southern Politics*.[13] Key provided a compelling account of racial politics in his demonstration that white racial hostility in the south varied as a function of black population concentrations within counties. The central thesis of *Southern Politics* was that the historical unfolding of southern politics depended on the relative dominance of white and black citizens in locally defined populations.[14] But in showing that racial hostility among whites was a direct function of local black population concentrations, how does Key escape his own indictment? What keeps politics in this analysis from becoming a socially determined side-show of social life more broadly defined?

Key sees racial conflict as the product of politics and purpose, where the interests of the participants in the conflict are locally defined. In his own words the central problem in the high black concentration counties was "the maintenance of control by a white minority."[15] In Key's analysis, political self-interest is used to explain racial hostility, even though racial hostility must still be understood with respect to a particular set of socially structured circumstances. Thus, the device that saves Key is individual purpose as it unfolds within a particular time and place. Key takes it as a given that, overall, whites in the postwar south had as a primary goal the maintenance of white political dominance.

The actions taken to realize this goal depended on situational specifics, however, the maintenance of white dominance was assumed in the hill country of Mississippi because there were very few blacks, but it was problematic in the delta where the concentration of black citizens was much higher. In summary, we see the merger of individual purpose and environmental circumstance quite early in the modern emergence of the political sociological tradition—a theme that is carried forward in more recent studies of the political consequences that arise due to the contexts and networks surrounding individual citizens.

Social Contexts

Understanding the politics of individual citizens within the political and social settings where they are located fits well within the political sociological traditions established by Key and Lazarsfeld and others. Indeed, a significant literature within modern voting studies addresses the contexts and networks of individual citizens—a literature inaugurated by the effects of Warren Miller and Robert Putnam.[16] While there is significant overlap in the study of contexts and networks, the fact remains that they present significantly different conceptual devices for understanding the impact of social structure on politics. More recent effects have provided a combined focus on the interplay between networks and contexts, but such a strategy requires that they be understood as separate constructs.

Social contexts are politically consequential because they influence the probabilities of social interaction within and across group boundaries, thereby affecting the social flow of politically relevant information. Hence, social contexts are perhaps best defined in terms of social composition, and in this sense, a context can be seen as the social composition of an environment.[17] The environment might be defined on varying bases—a dub, a neighbourhood, a church, a country, a province—and it has a multitude of defining properties. Some environments are old, big, geographically based, isolated, and attractive, while others are not. Similarly, the social context of an environment can be defined in terms of its various compositional properties—the proportion of inhabitants who are Social Democrats, liberals, Catholic, politically active, and well educated. Moreover, some efforts have been made to assess the consequences of heterogeneity within contexts, conceived as dispersion around a central compositional tendency.

Defined in this way, contexts lie beyond the reach of individual control—they are not manufactured by way of individual preference. This is not to say, however, that people do not locate themselves within particular contexts while they avoid others. Indeed, such locational decisions may be strategically motivated on the basis of social, political and economic criteria. The important point is, however, that once a person is located within a context, heroic efforts will be required to change the context. There are, of course, heroic exemplars: the party worker who delivers his or her precinct, the Jehovah's Witness canvasser who tries to convert his or her neighbourhood, and so on. But most of us probably take the contexts as given. Hence, absent the problem of self-selection, contexts are treated as exogenous to the actor.

When can the issue of self-selection be ignored? Most particularly, self-selection becomes a less plausible hypothesis when it involves large units of aggregation, when the motive underlying locational or membership choice is politically irrelevant, when the demonstration of contextual effects is linked empirically to a dynamic process, when the contextual effect is linked to a process of social or political conflict, and in general when a more sophisticated mechanism of contextual influence is specified. We consider each of these in turn.

First, consider the size of the aggregation unit. In a fascinating study, Erikson, Wright, and McIver have demonstrated the importance of state-level political cultures for the structure of political coalitions and the behaviour of individual voters.[18] There are a great many other reasons for rejecting self-selection arguments in their work, but at the most basic level, would we really expect that people locate themselves in states (or provinces or counties) for politically relevant reasons? As the units of aggregation become larger, the plausibility of self-selection as an account of contextual effects grows smaller.

Second, an increasing number of studies have turned toward the demonstration of contextual effects in time. Huckfeldt and Sprague[19] show that political campaigns enhance contextual effects—the effects are larger at the end of the campaign—and that the magnitude of the enhancement varies in systematic ways across different groups defined in terms of individual characteristics. Grofman *et al.* and Carmines *et al.*, show that the previously documented "Key effect" can be demonstrated in time.[20] Both efforts show that the white exodus from the Democratic Party has been accelerated by events of the 1960s in counties where black populations are most concentrated. Dynamic formulations such as these are quite difficult to recast in terms of a self-selection argument: do people relocate themselves between observations in a way that produces the spurious appearance of a time-structured effect?

Third, the "Key effect" is insulated from the self-selection argument on another basis as well. When a contextual effect is rooted in social or political hostility, self-selection once again lacks plausibility. If southern whites who live in black counties were racially hostile toward blacks, how can we lay the blame on self-selection? Do racially hostile whites locate in black counties in order to be near the objects of their hostility? In such an instance, the political behaviour is quite clearly predicated, in perhaps complex ways, on the surrounding social context.[21]

Finally, more sophisticated specifications of contextual influence tend in general to undermine the self-selection argument. One of the most important contributions in this regard was made by Erbring and Young, who argued that contextual effects should be seen as the endogenous feedbacks of behavioural interdependence.[22] In this same regard, Przeworski, Sprague and Westefield, Huckfeldt, and Przeworski and Sprague produced arguments that generally moved the contextual effects literature toward behavioural and informational interdependence as opposed to arguments rooted in shared social characteristics.[23] By focusing on socially communicated information and interdependent behaviour as the medium of contextual influence, the contextual effects literature has moved away from social reference group explanations for contextual influence. Consider Langton and Rapoport's explanation of support for Allende in 1964 among Santiago workers; workers who lived among other workers came to identify with these workers and hence to support Allende.[24] In spite of its attractiveness, such an explanation is vulnerable to the self-selection counter-explanation: only workers who identify as workers choose to live among workers.

As these more recent efforts suggest, there is more to the self-selection dispute than simple issues of temporal precedence. More fundamentally, these are debates regarding the role of individual purpose, the exogeneity of individual preferences, and the form of independent structural effects on individual behaviour. More complete specifications of contextual influence allow a reconciliation between individual purpose and the independent exogenous effect of social structure. But such an explanation typically involves a marriage between social contexts, social networks, and interdependent citizens who act purposefully on the basis of political goals. Finally, self-selection is not a repudiation of environmental influence. If people decide against joining the local Sierra Club chapter because it is full of knee-jerk environmentalists, it becomes difficult to suggest that political choice is independent of the social context. People choose to be part of some environments, and they avoid others, but neither choice is readily interpreted apart from the intersection of the individual and the environment.

Social Networks

While contexts are structurally defined and external to the individual, social networks are created as a consequence of individuals and their choices. Even though individuals may typically have little control over the political and social composition of their surroundings, they do exercise discretion over the networks of contacts they establish within various settings. In this way the social context serves as an environmental constraint on the individual—particularly on the individual's patterns of social interaction—and citizens make their choices among alternatives that are environmentally imposed. In some instances individual choice is swamped by these constraints. At a typical Peoria cocktail party, even committed socialists have little opportunity to talk politics with other socialists. Yet, in other instances, individual choice is imposed quite readily.

Consider the empirical results from Finigter's study of politics and the workplace,[25] where she examined the social interaction patterns of Detroit automobile workers at the factories where they were employed. The partisan composition of these factories was overwhelmingly Democratic, and the Democratic majority was relatively indiscriminate in their patterns of social interaction and association. In contrast, members of the Republican miniority were more likely to turn inward and form friendship groups which served as "protective environments for political deviants." (For parallel findings see Gans and Berger).[26] In short, members of the minority imposed their own political preferences on the social context in the creation of networks of social and political relations. In other words, social networks are created as the product of an intersection between the externally imposed social context and the citizen's own exogenous preference. And thus, at this particular level, social structure is neither deterministic nor a simple residue of individual preference.[27] Moreover, the exercise of individual choice in the construction of a network is contextually conditioned—minorities are more likely to be selective in their associational patterns.

Huckfeldt and Sprague engage in a series of analyses aimed at understanding the construction of social and political networks as a process that occurs through time, as individuals (1) realize repeated encounters within particular contexts and (2) make decisions regarding whether to convert these encounters into sources of political information.[28] Such a logic, which is inspired by the work of Coleman and McPhee *et al.*, takes account of both exogenous preference and independent, structurally imposed constraints on social interaction.[29] People do not roll over and accept whatever political information the environment happens to provide, but neither are they able to wholly escape the consequences of an environmentally supplied stream of information.

In keeping with Downs's early analysis, people reduce the costs of information by seeking out information sources that are biased in keeping with their own political preferences.[30] The extent to which individuals pursue such a strategy is likely to vary across individuals, depending on their sophistication, attentiveness, majority or minority standing, and so on. But one cannot avoid the conclusion that more politically sophisticated citizens should be more concerned to obtain biased information as opposed to information that is in some sense deemed to be politically objective—a conclusion that is in keeping with the analysis of Calvert.[31] In short, and perhaps ironically, information which carries a clearly understood political bias is more likely to be useful to the citizen.

Political preference is not determinate in the choice of information, however, because it operates within the context of an incoming information stream that is environmentally supplied. That is, the menu of choices lies beyond the control of the individual, and hence individual demand for information must be understood with respect to environmental supply. The key elements are two-fold. First, people select information sources on the basis of their own preferences. Second, the individual's set of informational alternatives reflects the bias of an environmental source. People are not unthinking products of their surroundings. Rather, their opinions become the complex products of environmentally biased information and their own pre-existing orientations.

The crucial element in recovering the independent citizen is recognising that both individual choice and the environmental supply of information operate probabilistically. The environment operates probabilistically because social contexts are seldom politically homogeneous. Even families disagree about politics, and hence people obtain information and viewpoints that reflect a less than determinate bias. If you live in a Democratic neighbourhood, you are more likely to see Democratic bumper stickers, but on occasion you will see one supporting a Republican candidate.

Why is choice probabilistic? First, individuals form social relationships based on a variety of preferences, not all of which can be easily realised in any single relationship. Moreover, many relationships are less than wholly specialised—we talk of politics, sports, and weather with overlapping sets of associates. Everything else being equal, Republican auto-workers would choose to eat lunch with another Republican, but everything else is not equal. If they are also fans of the Chicago Bears, they might prefer to avoid fans of the Detroit Lions, and it may be difficult to find a lunch partner who satisfies both preferences, particularly in a Detroit automobile factory. In other words, realising political preferences in the construction of a social network may be quite costly, particularly if multiple preferences are being realised in a single choice. Inevitably, people reduce their costs by compromising their preferences, and hence the control of information flow is incomplete.

Second, even if the Republican auto-worker is quite careful to avoid political conversation with a Democrat, a great deal of information is unsolicited—the person who works next to our Republican may wear a Democratic lapel pin. And hence, people are exposed to information inadvertently and unwillingly, and much of this exposure carries an environmental bias—people who work in banks see more Republican bumper stickers than people who work in automobile factories.

Finally, the choice of information sources is often incomplete because the underlying preference, upon which choice might be based, is uninformed. People often lack preferences, and thus they do not exercise informational control because they have no preference to use in arriving at selection criteria. Indeed, we are at the edge of a "catch-22" conundrum. I may wish to select information sources that are coincidental with my own political preferences, but how can I know what to prefer the absent necessary information? While information is often more useful if it carries an identifiable bias, there are times when people lack the necessary basis for either understanding or evaluating the bias that is carried.

Models of Influence

How are the political consequences of social and political structure realised? What are the mechanisms that tie together citizens with their surroundings? What are the alternative models of individual influence?

Methodological individualism lies at the core of the political sociological tradition, we are describing—individual citizens and their political choices constitute the primary objects of study.[32] The individual actor is not, however, seen in isolation, but rather in the context of surrounding constraints and opportunities that operate on patterns of social interaction, the acquisition of political information, and the formulation of political choice. At the same time, however, the individualistic impulse requires that the pathways of influence between the individual and the environment be clearly specified. It is not enough, in the case of Tingsten's Swedish workers, to show that those who live among other workers are more likely to vote for the Socialists.[33] The vehicle of influence must be specified as well. Did these workers vote for the socialists because they talked to their Socialist neighbours or because they talked to the local precinct worker? Why were the neighbours (or party workers) influential?

Hence, an important part of the sociological tradition revolves around the development, articulation, and evaluation of alternative models of influence—models of influence that place the individual at the center of the action. Not surprisingly, many of these models are derived from the political psychology and political economy traditions. And in this sense, the political sociological tradition has become agnostic with respect to epistemological issues regarding individual impulse—there is no official micro-theory that is inseparable from the political sociology tradition. This is not to say that any particular practitioner of the craft lacks an intellectual commitment to a particular individual-level model. Indeed, those who engage in multi-level analyses connecting citizens and environments include game theorists and cognitive psychologists, rational choice theorists and learning theorists. The tradition does not, however, necessarily dictate a micro-level motor that drives political and social processes. In other words, the political economist need not denounce rationality and rational actors to invoke a multi-level explanation because particular micro-sociological models might have roots that lie either in political psychology or in political economics.

The distinctive feature of micro-theory in the political sociological tradition is its purpose. The explanation of individual behaviour is not an end in itself, but rather a vehicle to attain a quite different goal—the explanation of interdependence among citizens and a more complete understanding of politics in its collective representations.[34] For political sociologists, the slippery slope of methodological individualism leads to methodological reductionism, and therein lies the anti-thesis of the political sociological tradition. A commitment to methodological individualism does not negate the sociological impulse, but an analysis that begins and ends either with the individual psyche or with an individual's rational calculation ceases to be sociological.

Boudon[35] argues for an individualistic tradition in sociology and a micro-sociological model that he traces to the work of

Weber.[36] The tradition is individualistic in its emphasis on individual purpose and individual motives, but it is sociological in its focus on the individually external factors that constrain individual behaviour. Hence, Boudon presents a micro-sociological model that places a (more or less) rational actor within a set of macro-sociological constraints.

Boudon's individualistic tradition might be illustrated quite well with developments in the models that seek to explain the nature of influence in social relationships. Particularly in the context of path-breaking family socialisation studies[37], it was perhaps natural for political scientists to adopt a model of social influence that was built upon intimacy and the interaction that occurs within cohesive social groups. The implicit or explicit assumption is that the influential communication of political information takes place between people who hold one another in high esteem and close personal regard, and these are the factors that make them trusted sources of political information and guidance. According to this view, intimacy and trust become the defining ingredients of political influence among citizens, and hence influence is unrelated to motive and purpose.

While this model was enhanced by the political socialisation studies, its history extends to an earlier period. Indeed, the Elmira and Erie County studies articulated social influence in terms which Burt calls the social cohesion model.[38] The social cohesion model portrays social influence in politics as occurring among people who hold each other in high personal regard and hence share a normative climate of opinion. Social influence becomes the by-product of close, intimate ties—citizens are more likely to influence one another to the extent that they hold each other in high personal regard, both as friends and as knowledgeable sources of political information.[39]

For many purposes, such a model may be entirely appropriate—there is no reason to expect that intimacy and cohesive social groups are unrelated to important forms of political influence. At the same time, the intimacy model may disregard important consequences that derive from the social communication of political information across the boundaries of social groups. Moreover, even the family socialisation studies have experienced difficulty in demonstrating the importance of intimacy to the flow of influential political communication.[40] Butt re-analyses evidence from the medical innovation study and calls into question the role of social communication through cliques and cohesive groups in encouraging doctors to adopt a new drug.[41] Huckfeldt and Sprague demonstrate that people engage in political discussion with others who are less than intimate associates, and intimacy does not necessarily translate into higher levels of influence.[42]

Findings such as these push for a reconstruction of the micro-theory of political influence arising through social communication. Burt advocates a structural equivalence model, conceived in terms of network ties.[43] Two individuals are structurally equivalent if they are similarly located in social structure—if, in network terms, they are connected to the same individuals in the same ways. In terms of politics, such a model might suggest that an individual's capacity for exercising influence is rooted in coincidental interests. One citizen is more likely to be influenced by another to the extent that the citizen being influenced recognises the existence of commonalties and shared interests, and hence the existence of a congenial bias.[44]

But the relevance of communication occurring across, the boundaries of cohesive social groups extends beyond the explanation of individual behaviour. If intimacy is a pre-condition for influence, then methodological reductionism is not seriously called into question as a method of political analysis. It only becomes important to relax the tightly constructed focus on individuals to incorporate a slightly expanded vision of the cohesive social cells that surround voters—their families and their most intimate associates. In contrast, if information is conveyed through less intimate social contacts, important implications arise for the nature and consequence of social communication in politics.

> First, if social communication beyond cohesive social groups is important, then the focus of political analysis can be profitably expanded to include the multiple and intersecting environments where social communication occurs—workplaces, neigh-bourhoods, and so on.
>
> Second, if important political communication occurs beyond the boundaries of cohesive groups, it becomes important to invoke Granovetter's analysis of weak ties.[45]

According to Granovetter, information that is communicated through weak ties travels more widely because it is less likely to feed back to the point of origin. Information obtained from one best friend is likely to be shared with another best friend, who is, in turn, quite likely to report it back to the source. Information obtained from a casual acquaintance might be shared with a second acquaintance, but it is unlikely to find its way back to the source because the source is less likely to be connected to the second acquaintance. As a consequence, information communicated through weak ties tends to spread and disseminate. In terms of politics, information communicated through weak ties is likely to create a public opinion that is more than a simple aggregation of individual opinions, but instead is a product of complex patterns of social communication.

In short, social communication that occurs through casual, less intimate social interaction is capable of creating a public opinion that is truly public—a public opinion that extends beyond the confines of individual calculation and cohesive social groups.[46] This is not to suggest that individuals play no role in these public opinion dynamics. Some citizens play more crucial roles than others in the dissemination of opinion, and an important task is the identification of these individuals. The important point for present purposes is that micro-theoretical constructs such as these have implications that extend beyond the explanation of individual behaviour to include the consequences of behavioural interdependence for the larger political community.

Psychological Responses to Political Research

Having seen that the model of the purposeful, instrumentally motivated citizen emerges quite clearly in a wide variety of sociologically oriented studies, we now show that the same citizen has been rediscovered by political psychologists in research as diverse as media studies, racial politics, and heuristically oriented political decision-making.

Media Effects

An important focus of the early Columbia studies was directed toward media effects on individual citizens and their choices. But after nearly twenty years of research, Klapper summarised the effort as the "minimal effects model."[47] Supporters of this general thesis have argued that the political impact of the media is likely to be attenuated for a variety of reasons:

(1) Citizens are not sufficiently attentive to be affected.

(2) Conflicting and intermittent messages tend to cancel out one other.

(3) Individual level processes—selective attention and retention based on pre-existing political predispositions—tend to distort media messages and hence nullify their effects.

(4) Any message that does leak through to the individual has been processed through patterns of social interaction and communication.

And thus, especially to the extent that patterns of social communication are contained within cohesive social groups that reflect an individual's own interests and characteristics, another element of the external political environment might be safely ignored.

Much of the early work on the media and media effects focused primarily on the political consequence of bias: How are people's political preferences altered by a biased media? Two interdependent processes—one at the level of individuals and the other at the level of the media—made the pursuit of bias effects a problematic undertaking. First, particularly in the United States, the media has self-consciously moved toward a politically detached and objective style of reporting. In practice, this has meant that the partisan press often has been replaced by an adversarial press.[48] Rather than continuing the 19th century role of partisan champion for particular candidates and parties, the modern press has created the role of the professional, politically detached, critical observer. Such a role frequently places the news media in an adversarial position with respect to both sides in partisan struggles. Indeed, we might argue that it creates a new bias—the bias of objectivity.

Second, and returning to our earlier discussion of the greater utility of biased information for sophisticated individuals, this trend has produced information that is frequently more costly and hence less useful for many citizens. If information without a well-understood bias is difficult to integrate and incorporate within political decision-making, then the modern media have become increasingly less relevant as they have become increasingly detached and adversarial. The modern newspaper, for example, finds itself in a position where it has no political following, but only an audience of political junkies who are willing and able to pay the high price of sifting, sorting, and evaluating the politically detached information that it presents. In other words, because the media have come to occupy a permanently adversarial position with respect to *all parties* in the political arena, the citizen cannot use the media as a cost-cutting source of information. And thus it is not surprising that the utility of media reports as sources of political information has tended to decline for many citizens, at the same time that the impact of the media on citizen viewpoints has been difficult to establish. In short, bias-free information is often less useful and hence less influential.

These problems are perhaps illustrated best in the work of Beck.[49] As he shows, Democratic partisans accuse the press of a Republican bias, and Republican partisans accuse the press of a Democratic bias. Such effects are particularly noteworthy because they operate in an opposite direction from the effects that arise on social communication. At the same time the citizens (often wrongly) project their own partisan preferences onto their associates, they also (often wrongly) project opposite preferences onto their newspapers. Quite clearly, the price of objectivity is an increase in the level of criticism from both partisan camps. If sophisticated citizens put a high value on information that comes with a well recognised political bias, such dissatisfaction is perhaps more easily understood. What is less understandable is why, in the modern media age, we should have developed such primitive expectations regarding media effects in the first place.

A significant stride forward in media research occurred when scholars began focusing more intently on agenda-setting.[50] Efforts aimed at understanding the political consequences of media coverage switched from media bias to media coverage, based on the insight that media influence is not simply a matter of telling people how to vote, but rather a matter of influencing citizen perceptions regarding the importance of various issues and problems. Stated quite simply, the argument suggests that issues covered by the media become the issues that citizens view as important, and hence the connection between the real objective political landscape of policy problems and issues, on the one hand, and people's perceptions of that landscape on the other, depends fundamentally on what the media chooses to report.

Erbring *et al.*, made a lasting contribution to the agenda-setting literature in their effort to demonstrate "audience-contingent media effects embedded in an issue specific micro model of salience."[51] They show that citizen perceptions of national problems include an important localised component that is explained on the basis of varying media reports. Even if the variability of local conditions is taken into account, the coverage of various policy problems by the local media has a pronounced impact on what citizens think is important. At the same time, they show that receptivity to the media agenda is "audience contingent"—it is dependent on people's own concerns and preferences.

This last point is especially important because it reinforces the emergent trend in political sociology—the intersection between environmentally supplied information and the preferences of individual citizens. In the case of social communication, citizens attempt to construct patterns of social interaction that minimize their exposure to disagreeable political messages, and in other instances socially communicated messages are either disguised or misperceived in ways that exaggerate agreement.[52] The exercise of citizen preference is more problematic in the case of the media for two reasons.

> First, only a very restricted range of alternative choices is typically available—very few citizens read any newspaper other than the locally supplied alternative.
>
> Second, even when more alternatives are available, such as the case of television news, they are typically quite homogeneous and uniform in the content of their coverage.

Nevertheless, individual preference is still invoked in the *interpretation* of environmentally supplied information: people develop a combative stance toward the media by imputing an unfavourable political bias. And they respond selectively to media coverage—they are not equally likely to think that all issues covered by the media are equally important.

Other subtle forms of media influence have been pursued in recent studies by Iyengar and Kinder and Iyengar.[53] In a series of carefully and creatively constructed experiments, Iyengar and Kinder examine not only the consequences of agenda-setting by the media, but also the impact of media "priming." Citizens are limited in the amount of information they can employ in rendering political judgments, and hence they make choices based on a limited number of concerns. Correspondingly, the crucial determinant of party and candidate success is often the sets of criteria used by citizens to make their political decisions, and Iyengar and Kinder establish the potential of the media to "prime" citizen decision-making by establishing the basis of evaluation. Once again, the results support the importance of an intersection between environmentally supplied information and the political preferences of those who are exposed to the information source. In the words of Iyengar and Kinder[54], "Priming is greatest when viewers are predisposed, by virtue of a well-developed, accessible theory, to see a connection between the president's responsibilities and the condition of the country." And for most citizens, this means that partisan preferences intersect with media reports to determine the extent of media priming effects.

In a sequel effort, Iyengar pursues the importance of media framing—media effects on the attribution of responsibility for policy problems.[55] He argues that television's primary mode of communication—episodic coverage of particular events—encourages the attribution of responsibility for policy problems to individuals rather than to larger social and political forces. As before, we see the importance of the intersection between citizen preference and predisposition on the one hand, and environmentally supplied information on the other. In particular, partisanship tends to limit the effects of framing. In his own words, "Individuals' partisan affiliations provide them an important resource with which to resist the suggestions of news frames".

The extent to which individual citizens play active or passive roles in the acquisition and interpretation of information from the media is open to alternative interpretations. Certainly Downs would ascribe an important role to individuals as they aggressively pursue the economies that derive from locating information sources that convey a compatible bias.[56] In contrast, Iyengar and Kinder see individuals as the victims of a media that lies beyond their control—two of their chapter titles describe citizens as the victims of agenda-setting and priming on the part of the media.[57] Regardless of the particular interpretation given to the role of citizens, media studies almost necessarily focus on the question of whether viewers respond to the media as purposeful, instrumentally motivated consumers of political information.

The Politics of Race

The emergent focus on this intersection between the individual and the environment is illustrated quite well with respect to several controversies in the literature on race and politics in the United States. In general, this literature aims to explain the source of racial conflict in politics. In particular, why and under what circumstances do white citizens demonstrate political preferences, choices, and behaviours that are hostile to black citizens?

The authors of this chapter have been involved in efforts aimed at connecting the politics of race to political and electoral change. Carmines and Stimson argue that the evolution of race is responsible for a transformation of American politics.[58] Beginning in the Congress, filtering through party organisations, and ultimately being demonstrated in elections and voter loyalties, the American political landscape has been reorganised in terms of race. Huckfeldt and Kohfeld argue that race has not only grown in importance, but its growth has led to a concomitant decline in the importance of class as an organising principle in contemporary American politics.[59] And thus the importance of class frequently has been eclipsed by the ascendancy of race as the primary line of cleavage in American elections.

These efforts share a common viewpoint in which race is understood as one among several possible lines of political conflict. And thus they might be subsumed under what Bobo and Glaser refer to as group conflict theories of racial hostility.[60] The underlying logic is that, under particular social, institutional, and environmental circumstances, race becomes crucial as a line of cleavage in politics. Racial politics is not, in short, something that simply occurs in the heads of voters. Instead it is a product of time, place, and circumstance, as a particular setting gives rise to the realisation of particularly defined interests and impulses. For Carmines and Stimson this means that the politics of race became ascendant as the result of political élites who chose a propitious moment to place the race issue on the political agenda. For

Huckfeldt and Kohfeld, this means that race typically grows more important when the political dominance of whites is numerically threatened by the presence of blacks, and when politicians construct coalitional appeals that successfully exploit the racial divide.

The first line of resistance to arguments such as these is the assertion that race does not matter, or at least that the political importance of race is radically overstated. The most recent advocate of this position is Abramowitz[61] who writes in response to Carmines and Stimson.[62] The general line of argument, which was offered earlier in the work of Wolfinger and Arseneau, is that racial attitudes do a poor job in explaining partisanship differences or voting choices once the effects of other policy opinions are taken into account.[63] Hence, people's attitudes toward civil rights are independent of partisan choice.

Several responses are available to the "race does not matter" critique. One response, rooted in cognitive political psychology, argues that for many voters a broad range of issue opinions are organised cognitively with respect to race, and hence race tends to permeate a diverse range of public policy concerns.[64] A second response, rooted in the political sociology of race, argues that the "race does not matter" critique fails the macro-political reality check. If the political consequences of race do not matter, why do 90 percent of voting blacks regularly support Democratic candidates for the presidency, while a majority of voting whites have supported Republican presidential candidates in every election since 1964?

Even among those who accept the premise that race *does* matter, there is significant disagreement regarding the nature of racial effects in politics. Group conflict theorists argue that racial politics is the result of political competition between whites and blacks over scarce resources, and hence is rooted in reality-based assessments on the part of political actors. In contrast, the symbolic racism thesis argues that racial conflict is, in fact, divorced from reality—from the real circumstances and interests of the actors. Rather, racial conflict is rooted in prejudice and hostility toward blacks, and hence it is stimulated and manipulated on the basis of symbolic issues and appeals.[65]

Our goal here is not to take sides in these debates—we occupy such an intellectually partisan role in other places! Rather our purpose is to demonstrate the roots of these alternative explanations with respect to enduring traditions in political behaviour research. Group conflict theories of racial conflict lie in the mainstream of a tradition in political sociology that conceives of macro-political outcomes at the intersection between individual purpose and orientation on the one hand, and the political and social environment on the other. The other two arguments—"race does not matter" and "racial conflict is the same as prejudice"—are both rooted in individualistic conceptions of political behaviour and traditions that seek the explanation of macro-political outcomes in terms of either wholly individualistic impulses or wholly internalised cultural norms. Notice that the group conflict thesis is essentially noncommittal with respect to the role played by prejudice in racial conflict. Advocates of the group conflict position might argue either that prejudice plays a crucial role in the dynamic of racial conflict, or that it plays a minor role. What the group conflict position *does* argue is that prejudice alone is not an adequate explanation of racial conflict—racial conflict might exist quite apart from prejudice and, alternatively, prejudice might exist quite apart from racial conflict.

Heuristically Guided Political Decision-making

It is not news that most citizens have only limited knowledge and information about politics and public affairs. While a minority of citizens are well informed, a majority—and by many accounts, a large majority—lack information about basic facts, salient issues, and significant political figures. If most citizens lack such elementary political information, how can they act as effective political participants? Indeed, how can they formulate meaningful political opinions? And yet plainly most citizens do have political opinions and express them on a vast array of political topics. Moreover, although these attitudes obviously do not represent reasoned judgments logically derived from full-blown and well-articulated philosophical premises, neither are they capricious or whimsical. Most people seemingly know why they prefer one policy position over another, and this provides at least the potential for effective political action. How is this possible, given their lack of attention to politics and their paucity of information about public affairs?

Anthony Downs was the first analyst to give serious attention to the problem of political information in modern mass democracies.[66] Reasoning that the costs of becoming informed about the details of political issues generally outweigh the relative benefits to be derived from voting on an informed basis, he argues that it is irrational for most citizens to become fully knowledgeable about public affairs. Downs identifies three types of costs involved in becoming informed:[67]

(1) Procurement costs are the costs of gathering, selecting, and transmitting data.

(2) Analysis costs are the costs of undertaking a factual analysis of data.

(3) Evaluative costs are the costs of relating data or factual analysis to specific goals, *i.e.*, of evaluating them.

Together, these costs constitute a formidable barrier to becoming political informed—too formidable. Downs argues, for most citizens rationally to invest the time, attention, and resources needed to become politically informed. Rather, rational citizens have strong incentives to develop methods of avoiding the substantial costs of information acquisition. They do so by developing a variety of short-cuts in the gathering and use of information. These shortcuts allow citizens to make political decisions and form political preferences without becoming fully informed about the content and details of political issues. In short, their use leads to minimally informed—but informed nonetheless—citizenry.

Since Downs wrote so insightfully about the rational basis of political ignorance, a large literature in cognitive and social psychology focusing on decision-making under conditions of complexity and uncertainty has emerged.[68]

Beginning with Tversky and Kahneman's highly influential paper, this work has disclosed that individuals use a wide variety of heuristics— that is, cognitive shortcuts that reduce complex problem-solving to more simple judgmental operations—to make many social decisions.[69]

Kahneman and Tversky have identified four fundamental heuristic principles that allow individuals to focus on a limited set of information to make decisions rather than engaging in a detailed analysis of all available information. These principles are availability, representativeness, adjustment, and simulation. Briefly, availability refers to the salient features of a decision-making situation, so that individuals need not attend to all available or even relevant information. For example, in deciding whether to identify oneself as a liberal, citizens may focus only on the most prominent liberal spokesman such as Senator Kennedy or Jesse Jackson rather than considering all those political figures and organisations that call under the liberal category. Representativeness focuses on the probability that an item or piece of information is part of the appropriate class of all information. Thus, representativeness bears on the typicality of information—whether it possesses the central or defining properties of a given class of information. A representative heuristic principle would be invoked, for example, if a voter relied on the race of the candidate in a congressional contest between an African-American and a white to estimate which candidate is the Democrat (or Republican). In a racially contested election, African Americans are far more likely to be Democrats than Republicans while whites are just as likely to be Republicans. The fact that this is not invariably the case only shows that no heuristic principle, including representativeness, can be employed without a certain probability of error.

The final two heuristic principles discussed by Kahneman and Tversky involve more cognitive processing than either the availability or representativeness principles. The adjustment principle refers to the changes that are made in decisions after making an initial, tentative response. The initial or anchoring response is adjusted as relevant new information is brought to bear on the decision. Thus, in estimating the political ideology of a candidate it might be useful to know that she/he is a Democrat and therefore, more likely to be a liberal based on this initial piece of information. But this initial estimate might very well be adjusted if it turns out the candidate opposes all abortions, supports the death penalty, and favours a strict balanced budget. In other words, the anchoring estimate is altered as more relevant information becomes available.

The final heuristic principle studied by Kahneman and Tversky involves still more cognitive processing by the decision-maker. The simulation heuristic comes into play when relevant information is lacking and the individual must try to anticipate the consequences of a given decision scenario. In deciding whether to support a given military project, the Secretary of Defense attempts to decide whether the project is feasible, effective, and worth the investment in terms of providing greater security to the nation. Notice that existing information is only of limited value in this situation because the crucial factor is the probable reaction of your potential adversaries—thus highlighting the substantial amount of cognitive processing involved in the application of the simulation heuristic.

Applications of heuristics in political psychology do not usually make use of the specific heuristic principles discussed by Kahneman and Tversky but rather specific political heuristics felt to be more relevant to political decision-making. Yet some of these heuristics can be usefully interpreted within the Kahneman—Tverksy framework. The use of stereo-types to make political judgments, for example, clearly involves the application of the representative heuristic. Poor people, for example, may be seen as lazy and irresponsible—those undeserving of governmental assistance. Alternatively, they may be viewed as hard-working and responsible but unable to find appropriate jobs; this perception is likely to foster greater support for governmental employment programmes. Thus, stereo-typical judgments are based on the essential or defining features of a group—their representativeness.

Brady and Sniderman discuss what they term a likability heuristic.[70] This heuristic enables citizens to make inferences about the issue orientations of various political groups. The authors reason that if citizens have an opinion on a given political issue and have affective evaluations of various political groups, then they will attribute their opinion to favoured groups, and the opposite opinion to disfavoured groups. This turns out to lead to fairly accurate estimates of the issue stands of specific political groups—even though many citizens lack detailed information of the groups' issue positions.

As Mondak has noted, Brady and Sniderman's likability heuristic can be viewed as an application of the adjustment heuristic.[71] The individual's own issue position provides an anchoring for the estimated position of the particular group. Additional information—specifically, their affective evaluation of political groups—leads to the estimates of their issue positions. And this estimate is adjusted as new information becomes available.

Both Carmines and Kuklinski and Mondak discuss what may be termed source cues, a particularly important decision heuristic for politically inattentive and uninformed citizens.[72] Their studies show that citizens, in formulating policy assessments and even in developing their own policy position, often rely on prominent political figures. Thus, attributing the defense buildup in the 1980s to President Reagan, affected citizens' evaluation of that policy but only among respondents who lacked detailed policy information. Similarly, the experimental studies conducted by Carmines and Kuklinski indicate that citizens are more likely to form their own opinion on issues if salient political leaders (i.e., Senators Kennedy or Helms) are identified either as proponents or opponents of the issue proposal.[73]

By using heuristic principles we see how citizens can make relatively informed judgments about politics on the basis of limited—even minimal—information. In the process, we also see how new developments in political psychology have helped re-establish the role of the citizenry as purposeful, instrumentally motivated actors in the political process.

Converging Models of Democratic Citizens in Political Behaviour

In answering the fundamental challenge of the democratic citizen embedded in the political economy tradition, political behaviour research—and, indeed, political science—has come closer to defining a distinctively political model of citizenship. The strategic actor found in the political economy tradition has re-appeared in the political sociology and political psychology traditions. In the process, a convergence has emerged among these three traditions in the resulting model of democratic citizenship that they propose. The core of this convergence lies in a model of citizens who act purposefully on the basis of their own goals, ambitions, and needs.

We are intentionally avoiding the "r" word, and many political economists will not be satisfied with the implementation of citizen purpose as it is typically employed in studies of political behaviour. At the same time, a great many students of political behaviour have come to accept something that approaches Popkin's description of the reasoning voter:[74] "They think about who and what political parties stand for; they think about the meaning of political endorsements; they think about what government can and should do. And the performance of government, parties, and candidates affects their assessments and preferences." Moreover, and as Popkin points out, such reasoning is accomplished on the basis of "low information rationality"—short-cut methods of collecting and processing information about politics.

Perhaps the major controversy surrounding the conception of purposeful citizens concerns whether such a model of instrumental behaviour has any real analytic consequence. That is, how much analytic purchase has been obtained by beginning with the assumption that citizens act instrumentally on the basis of their own purposes? According to Simon, the assumption (or acknowledgment) of rationality yields very modest analytic reward—simply asserting that citizens are rational takes us very little distance toward a convincing political analysis.[75] Rather, a series of auxiliary assumptions must be made in order to generate analytic utility from the assumption of instrumental citizen behaviour, and it is at this point that the analysis truly begins.[76]

The auxiliary assumptions are important for a variety of reasons. First, they provide meaning to the model of purposeful citizens and instrumental behaviour. One model of purposeful citizens generates analytic utility by suggesting that citizens update their assessments of parties and politicians by reviewing past experience.[77] Another model suggests that instrumental citizens reduce information costs by obtaining information from other citizens. Still another model suggests that citizens reduce their information costs through a series of analytic short-cuts, or heuristics.[78] These analyses, and many more, are at least partially motivated by the assumption that citizens act in reasonable ways to realize their goals. But beyond that point, they may be radically dissimilar in the models of citizen decision-making that they put forward.

Moreover, while the concept of citizen purpose may lie beyond the reach of direct empirical scrutiny, the auxiliary assumptions are often subject to the bright light of empirical evaluation. Thus, the premise of citizen purpose does not mean much until we determine how citizen's purposes are realised. Therein lies, for example, the contribution of Fiorina's retrospective voting model: it articulates the consequences of purposeful citizens at the same time that it provides a basis for empirical evaluation.

Indeed, a great deal of contemporary research in political behaviour is concerned with working out the consequences of citizen purpose. The work of Snidernan *et al.*, provides an exemplar of this general research programme[79]: his focus on the manner in which citizens reason about their choices and his articulation of "reasoning chains" are some of the ways that the concept of citizen purpose is given meaning. In short, the citizenship challenge posed by political psychology has been answered, in large part, by turning the challenge on its head. Rather than focusing on how much citizens fail to know about politics, the new look examines the way in which citizens quite sensibly attempt to contain the costs of acquiring and processing political information.

We might also suggest that a "new look" pervades a great deal of political sociology research as well. Rather than focusing on the extent to which individuals are reflections of the environments and contexts and groups within which they are embedded, the new look examines the manner in which citizen purpose is realised or thwarted within particular configurations of time, place, and setting. Rather than seeing individual behaviour as a straightforward product of exogenous determinants, citizen choices are seen as being interdependent with their surroundings. At the same time that preferences are informed by information taken from an environmentally determined supply, citizens also impress their preferences on the environment by way of their own information sampling criteria. In short, political information is obtained at the intersection between individually defined citizen purpose and environmentally determined information supply.

Perhaps unintentionally, students of political economy produced a citizenship challenge which ultimately provided part of the solution to companion challenges posed by political psychology and political sociology. By recognising the costs as well as the benefits of citizenship, the evolving analysis of political behaviour sees many old problems in a new light. In the attempt to come to grips with citizens who were neither independent nor well informed, a revised model of citizenship has emerged—a model of the citizen as a cost-conscious consumer and processor of political information who, while taking her duties seriously, has successfully reduced the impulse to be consumed by politics and political affairs. The end product is a more realistic view of citizenship and citizens in democratic politics—a view which understands citizens in the contexts of the real-world constraints imposed by their own inherent limitations as collectors and processors of political information. In many ways, this revised view of the citizen is not only more realistic but also more political, organised around a view of interests and information that is located in the characteristics not only of individuals, but also of the groups and settings to which they belong.

E.G. Carmines • R. Huckfeldt

REFERENCES

1. A. Campbell, P.E. Converse, W.E. Miller, and D.E. Stokes, *The American Voter*, New York: Wiley, 1960.
2. A. Downs, *An Economic Theory of Democracy*, New York: Harper and Row, 1957.
3. *Ibid.*
4. M. Olson, *The Logic of Collective Action*, Cambridge, Mass.: Harvard University Press, 1965.
5. E. Ostrom, *Governing the Commons*, New York: Cambridge University Press, 1990.
6. D. Knoke, *Political Networks*, New York: Cambridge University Press, 1990; D. Chong, *Collective Action and the Civil Rights Movement*, Chicago: University of Chicago Press, 1991.
7. J.H. Aldrich, "Rational choice and turnout", *American Journal of Political Science*, 37, 1993, pp. 246–78; R.W. Jackman, "Response to Aldrich's rational choice and turnout: rationality and political participation", *American Journal of Political Science*, 37, 1993, pp. 279–90.
8. M.P. Fiorina, "Information and rationality in elections", *Information and Democratic Processes*, ed. J.A. Ferejohn and J.H. Kuklinski, Urbana: University of Illinois Press, 1990, pp. 329–42.
9. H.A. Simon, *Models of Man*, New York: Wiley, 1957.
10. W.N. McPhee, R.B. Smith, and J. Ferguson, "A theory of informal social influence", *Formal Theories of Mass Behavior*, ed. W.N. McPhee, New York: Free Press, 1963, pp. 74–103.

11. P.F. Lazarsfeld, B. Berselson, and H. Gaudet, *The People's Choice*, New York: Columbia University Press, 1944, p. 27.
12. Jr. V.O. Key, and F. Munger, "Social determinism and electoral decision: The case of Indiana", *American Voting Behavior*, ed. by E. Burdick and A.J. Brodbeck, Glencoe, Ill.: Free Press, 1959, pp. 281–99.
13. Jr. V.O. Key, F. Munger, and H. Heard, *Southern Politics*, New York, Alfred A. Knopf, 1949.
14. D.R. Matthews, and J.W. Prothro, "Social and economic factors and negro voter registration in the South", *American Political Science Review*, 57, 1963, pp. 24–44; Jr. G.C. Wright, "Community structure and voting in the South", *Public Opinion Quarterly*, 40, 1976, pp. 200–15; M.W. Giles, and A. Evans, "External threat, perceived threat, and group identity", *Social Science Quarterly*, 66, 1985, pp. 50–66; R. Huckfeldt and C. Kohfeld, *Race and the Decline of Class in American Politics*, Urbana: University of Illinois Press, 1989; J.E. Alt, "The impact of the Voting Rights Act on Black and White voter registration in the South", *Quiet Revolution in the South: The Impact of the Voting Rights Act 1965–1990*, ed. C. Davison and B. Grofman. Princeton, N.J.: Princeton University Press, 1994, pp. 351–77.
15. Jr. V.O. Key, F. Munger, and H. Heard, *op. cit.*, 1949, p. 5.
16. W.E. Miller, "One-party politics and the voter", *American Political Science Review*, 50, 1956, pp. 707–25.
17. H. Eulau, *Politics, Self, and Society*, New York: Cambridge University Press, 1986.
18. R.S. Erikson, G.C. Wright, and J.P. McIver, *Statehouse Democracy: Public Opinion and Policy in the American States*, New York: Cambridge University Press, 1993.
19. R. Huckfeldt and J. Sprague, "Social order and political chaos: the structural setting of political information", *Information and Democratic Processes*, ed. J.A. Ferejohn and J. H. Kuklinski, Urbana: University of Illinois Press, 1990, pp. 23–58; *Citizens, Politics, and Social Communication*, New York: Cambridge University Press, 1995.

20. B. Grofman, L. Handley, and A. Glazer, "Modeling the link between race and electoral change using aggregate data", Mimeo., University of California, Irvine, 1993; E.G. Carmines, and C. McCurley, "Mobilization, countermobilization, and the politics of race", *Political Geography*, 14, 1995, pp. 601–19.

21. R. Huckfeldt, *Politics in Context: Assimilation and Conflict in Urban Neighborhoods*, New York: Agathon, 1986; R. Huckfeldt and C. Kohfeld, *op. cit.*, 1989.

22. L. Erbring, and A.A. Young, "Individuals and social structure: contextual effects as endogenous feedback", *Sociological Methods and Research*, 7, 1979, pp. 396–430.

23. A. Przeworksi, "Contextual models of political behaviour", *Political Methodology*, 1, 1974, pp. 27–61; J. Sprague, and L.P. Westefield, "An interpretive reconstruction of some aggregate models of contextual effects", Presented at the annual meeting of the Southern Political Science Association, Gatlinburg, November 1–3, 1979; R. Huckfeldt, "Social contexts, social networks, and urban neighbourhoods: environmental constraints on friendship choke", *American Journal of Sociology*, 89, 1983, pp. 651–69; "Political loyalties and social class ties: the mechanisms of contextual influence", *American Journal of Political Science*, 28, 1984, pp. 399–417; A. Przeworksi, and J. Sprague, *Paper Stones*, Chicago: University of Chicago Press, 1986.

24. K.P. Langton, and R. Rapoport, "Social structure, social context, and partisan mobilization: urban workers in Chile", *Comparative Political Studies*, 8, 1975, pp. 318–44.

25. A. Finifter, "The friendship group as a protective environment for political deviants", *American Political Science Review*, 68, 1974, pp. 607–25.

26. H.J. Gans, *The Levittowners*, New York: Vintage, 1967; B.M. Berger, *Working-Class Suburb*, Berkeley: University of California Press, 1960.

27. R. Boudon, *Theories of Social Change*, Berkeley: University of California Press, 1986.

28. R. Huckfeldt and J. Sprague, "Networks in context: the social flow of political information", *American Political Science Review*, 93, 1987, pp. 1197–216; "Choice, social structure, and political information:

the informational coercion of minorities", *American Journal of Political Science*, 32, 1988, pp. 467–82; Huckfeldt, R., *op. cit.*, 1983; 1986.

29. J.S. Coleman, *Introduction to Mathematical Sociology*, New York: Free Press, 1964; W.N. McPhee, R.B. Smith, and J. Ferguson, *op. cit.*, 1963.
30. A. Downs, *op. cit.*, 1957.
31. R.C. Calvert, "The value of biased information: a rational choice model of political advice", *Journal of Politics*, 4, 1985, pp. 530–55.
32. A. Przeworksi, "Marxism and rational choice", *Politics and Society*, 14, 1985, pp. 379–409.
33. H. Tingsten, *Political Behavior: Studies in Election Statistics*, trans. V. Hammarling, Totowa, N.J.: Bedminster, originally published 1937; rpt. 1963.
34. H. Eulau, *op. cit.*, 1986.
35. R. Boudon, *op. cit.*, 1986.
36. M. Weber, "On the concept of sociology and the meaning of social conduct", *Basic Concepts in Sociology*, trans. H.P. Secher, New York: Citadel Press; originally published 1925, ch.1 of *Wirtschaft und Gesellschaft*, 1966, pp. 29–58.
37. M.K. Jennings, and R.G. Niemi, *The Political Character of Adolescence*, Princeton, N.J.: Princeton University Press, 1974; M.K. Jennings, and R.G. Niemi, *Generations and Politics: A Panel Study of Young Adults and Their Parents*, Princeton, N.J.: Princeton University Press, 1981.
38. R.S. Burt, "Social contagion and innovation: cohesion versus structural equivalence", *American Journal of Sociology*, 92, 1987, pp. 1287–335.
39. E. Katz, "The two-step flow of political information: an up-to-date report on a hypothesis", *Public Opinion Quarterly*, 21, 1957, pp. 61–78.
40. M.K. Jennings, and R.G. Niemi, *op. cit.*, 1974; 1981; K.L. Tedin, "The influence of parents on the political attitudes of adolescents", *American Political Science Review*, 68, 1974, pp. 579–92.
41. J.S. Coleman, E. Katz, and H. Menzel, *Medical Innovation: A Diffusion Study*, Indianapolis, Ind.: Bobbs-Merrill, 1966.

42. R. Huckfeldt, and J. Sprague, "Discussant effects on vote choice: intimacy, structure, and interdependence", *Journal of Politics*, 53, 1991, pp. 122–58.

43. R.S. Burt, *op.cit.*, 1987.

44. A. Downs, *op. cit.,* 1957; R. Huckfeldt, and J. Sprague, *op. cit.,* 1991.

45. M. Granovetter, "The strength of weak ties", *American Journal of Sociology*, 78, 1973, pp. 1360–80.

46. J.A. Stimson, *Public Opinion in America: Moods Cycles and Swings*, Boulder, Colo.: Westview Press, 1991; M.B. MacKuen, R. Erickson, and J. Stimson, "Macropartisanship", *American Political Science Review*, 83, 1989, pp. 1125–45.

47. J.T. Klapper, *The Effects of Mass Communication*, New York: Free Press, 1960.

48. S. Iyengar, and D.R. Kinder, *News that Matters*, Chicago: University of Chicago Press, 1987.

49. P.A. Beck, "Voters' intermediation environments in the 1988 presidential contest", *Public Opinion Quarterly*, 55, 1991, pp. 371–94.

50. L. Erbring, E.N. Goldenberg, and A.H. Miller, "Front-page news and real-world cues: a new look at agenda setting by the media", *American Journal of Political Science*, 24, 1980, pp. 16–49; M.B. MacKuen, "Social communication and the mass policy agenda", *More than News*, ed. M. MacKuen and S.L. Coombs, Beverly Hills, California: Sage, 1981, pp. 19–146.

51. L. Erbring, E.N. Goldenberg, and A.H. Miller, *op. cit.*, 1980, p. 21.

52. M.B. MacKuen, "Speaking of politics: individual conversational choice, public opinion, and the prospects for deliberative democracy", *Information and Democratic Processes*, ed. J.A. Ferejohn and J.H. Kuklinski, Urbana: University of Illinois Press, 1990, pp. 59–99.

53. D.R. Kinder, *op. cit.,* 1987; S. Iyengar, *Is Anyone Responsible?* Chicago: University of Chicago Press, 1991.

54. D.R. Kinder, *op. cit.,* 1987.

55. S. Iyengar, *op. cit.,* 1991.
56. A. Downs, *op. cit.,* 1957.
57. S. Iyengar and D.R. Kinder, *op. cit.,* 1987.
58. E.G. Carmines, and J.A. Stimson, *Issue Evolution: Race and the Transformation of American Politics*, Princeton, N.J.: Princeton University Press, 1989.
59. R. Huckfeldt, and C. Kohfeld, *op. cit.*, 1989.
60. L. Bobo, "Whites' opposition to busing: symbolic racism or realistic group conflict?", *Journal of Personality and Social Psychology*, 45, 1983, pp. 1196–210; J.M. Glaser, "Back to the black belt: racial environment and white racial attitudes in the South", *Journal of Politics*, 56, 1994, pp. 21–41.
61. A.J. Abramowitz, "Issue evolution reconsidered: racial attitudes and partisanship in the US electorate", *American Journal of Political Science*, 38, 1994, pp. 1–24.
62. J.A. Stimson, *op. cit.*, 1989.
63. R.E. Wolfinger, and R.B. Arsenau, "Partisan change in the South, 1952–1976", *Political Parties: Development and Decay*, ed. L. Maisel and J. Cooper, Beverly Hills, California: Sage, 1978, pp. 179–210.
64. R. Hamill, M. Lodge, and F. Blake, "The breadth, depth, and utility of class, partisan, and ideological schemata", *American Journal of Political Science*, 29, 1985, pp. 850–70.
65. D.O. Sears, C.P. Hensler, and L.K. Speer, "Whites, opposition to busing, self-interest or symbolic politics?", *American Political Science Review*, 73, 1979, pp. 369–84.
66. A. Downs, *op. cit.,* 1957.
67. *Ibid.*, p. 210.
68. V.C. Ottati, and Jr. R.S. Wyer, "The cognitive mediators of political choice: toward a comprehensive model of political information processing", *Information and Democratic Process*, ed. J.A. Ferejohn and J.H. Kuklinski, Urbana: University of Illinois Press, 1990, pp. 186–216.

69. A. Tversky, and D. Kahneman, "Judgment under uncertainty, heuristics and biases", *Science*, 185, 1974, pp. 1124–31.
70. H.E. Brady, and P.M. Sniderman, "Attitude attribution: a group basis for political reasoning", *American Political Science Review*, 79, 1985, pp. 1061–78; P.M. Sniderman, R.A. Brody, and P.E. Tetlock, *Reasoning and Choice*, New York: Cambridge University Press, 1991.
71. J.J. Mondak, "Cognitive heuristics, heuristic processing, and efficiency in political decision making", *Research in Micropolitics*, Vol. IV, ed. M.X. Delli Cappini, L. Huddy and R.Y. Shapiro, Greenwich, Conn.: JAI Press, 1994, pp. 117–41.
72. E.G. Carmines, and J.H. Kuklinski, "Incentives, opportunities, and the logic of public opinion in American political representation", *Information and Democratic Process*, ed. J.A. Ferejohn and J.H. Kuklinski, Urbana: University of Illinois Press, 1990, pp. 240–68; J.J. Mondak, "Source cues and policy approval: the cognitive dynamics of public support for the Reagan agenda", *American Journal of Political Science*, 37, 1993, pp. 186–212.
73. E.G. Carmines, and J.H. Kuklinski, *op. cit.*, 1990.
74. S.L. Popkin, *The Reasoning Voter: Communication and Persuasion in Presidential Campaigns*, Chicago: University of Chicago Press, 1991, p. 7.
75. H.A. Simon, "Human nature in politics: the dialogue of psychology with political science", *American Political Science Review*, 79, 1985, pp. 293–304.
76. M. Lodge, and R. Hamill, "A partisan schema for political information processing", *American Political Science Review*, 80, 1986, pp. 505–19; M. Lodge, and R. Hamill, K.M. McGraw, and P. Stroh, "An impression-driven model of candidate evaluation", *American Political Science Review*, 83, 1989, pp. 399–419.
77. M.P. Fiorina, *Retrospective Voting in American National Elections*, New Haven, Conn.: Yale University Press, 1981.
78. P.M. Sniderman, R.A. Brody, and P.E. Tetlock, *Reasoning and Choice*, New York: Cambridge University Press, 1991.
79. *Ibid.*

❑❑❑

2

Reasoning Voters and Multi-party Systems

Studying political behaviour at the level of the general electorate has changed considerably from the early days, characterised by the predominance of the Michigan model in the 1960s[1] and the juxtaposition of this social-psychological approach with the rational choice approach of Downs.[2] Beginning with revisionist arguments in favour of issue voting[3], and continuing through both traditional and rational choice ideas about retrospective voting, a concept of the "reasoning voter" has emerged.[4]

This concept functions as a bridge between political psychologists and "realist" versions of the rational choice approach —versions which try to predict actual voting behaviour, instead of focusing exclusively on equilibrium conditions for the demand and supply of policy packages. Reasoning voters are approximately rational, trying to come to terms with a decision situation about which they are only vaguely informed. Judgmental heuristics are used to solve "Simon's puzzle" of how to decide rationally "with limited information and processing capacity".[5]

Within a rational choice framework, Popkin adopts the term "reasoning voter" to describe a similar situation in which "voters actually do reason about parties, candidates, and issues"[6], "investing" their vote in collective goods on the basis of "costly and imperfect information under conditions of uncertainty".[7] As contrasted with private investors, these "public investors" have less incentive to gather costly information. Hence Popkin characterises this choice situation as one of low-cost rationality, where the premium is on gathering inexpensive information from friends and using informational and calculative short-cuts.

Concept of the Reasoning Votes

The general insight contained in the concept of the reasoning voter is not new. Since the original *homo economicus* was gradually turned into a utility maximizer, subjectively calculating the probabilities of outcomes, it was only a small step to realize that the acquisition of perfect information is often too expensive (a point already present in Downs).[8] What is new is that cognitive psychology can now offer a set of experimentally tested results: about "schemata" for acquiring, processing and retrieving information; about dominant "frames" simplifying the goal structure; and about habits as quick decision rules in frequently recurring decision situations.[9]

These theories enable the cognitive psychologist to model individual decision-making. But in political science in general, and in voting research in particular, it is also necessary to consider the interface between the choices of individuals and the world of party politics and government policy. This chapter focuses on problems of preference formation and party choices of reasoning voters in multi-party systems. This is a necessary and separate task, in a field where the research agenda focuses heavily on the American two-party system and its presidential elections.

Rational choice is behaviour which is consistent with one's preferences, the preferences themselves having to fulfill minimal conditions of consistency such as transitivity and so on. Thus, we will first consider problems of party preferences of voters in multi-party systems. Second, the forces influencing these preferences are taken into account. Building on the concept of the reasoning voter, we shall consider how variables like issue proximities, retrospective evaluations of government performance and party identification can be interpreted in a model of preference formation in multi-party systems. The final task will be to analyze the decision problem itself, taking into account future expectations about possible government coalitions, incentives for sophisticated voting and instrumental versus expressive or symbolic voting.

The overall model of this chapter is built on the assumption that, in multi-party systems, voters' party preference profiles are the crucial link between the factors influencing reasoning about parties and the final voting decision. In this sense, "party preference" has an analogous causal status as "comparative candidate evaluations" in the revised Michigan model.[10] From among possible influences on party preference, issue proximities and retrospective evaluations are identified as factors most proximate to the process of preference formation in the assumed funnel of causality. Issue proximities constitute a substantive prospective measure, while retrospective evaluations pertain to the past performance of the present government. Future expectations are more difficult to integrate in models for multi-party systems, since the future government depends not only on election results but also on future coalition-building. Coalition expectations influence the final decision outcome, insofar as the voter has to reason about the government which will be a possible consequence of the various different ways of casting his or her vote which are compatible with his or her party preference profile.

This chapter touch upon what Huckfeldt and Carmines call the "economists' challenge" to sociological and social psychological approaches to the study of voting behaviour. Purposeful, rational action has as its pre-condition clear preferences and reasoning about the consequences of one's action. This latter task is complicated when the outcome which counts is the aggregate of all people's votes rather than the result of one individual's action alone. In discussion of preference formation takes up political psychological concerns about the process of becoming informed, thus rendering possible the matching of personal goals with the party-political means of achieving those goals.

Party Preferences in Multi-Party Systems

In a two-party system, the relation between party preference and party choice is rather simple, once the voter has decided to participate in an upcoming election at all. Either a voter prefers party or candidate *A*, in which case s/he will choose this alternative; or else s/he prefers party or candidate *B* and will, therefore, choose that alternative; and indifference should lead to abstention. It would be irrational, in a two-party setting, to vote for a party which is not one's first choice.

The choice problem in a three-party system is not a straightforward extrapolation of the two-party case. There, it may be rational to vote strategically for one's second most preferred party if one expects one's most preferred party to lose and one's least preferred party otherwise to win. The strict preference order between three parties contains 3! = 6 logical possibilities, and even more if ties of two or all three parties are contemplated. With three possible answers to every paired comparison between three parties (counting pairs for the same parties only once, not twice as ordered pairs), there exist 27 different possible preference orderings; among the 13 consistent individual rank orders, one profile has all three parties tied, six preference profiles have two-parties tied at either the first or last rank, and another six constitute strict rank orders. From three parties upward, it is no longer self-evident that voters have consistent preferences.

Ideally, one would hope that the preferences of individual voters are consistent enough for them to be expressed in a precise utility function which is not just the trivial outcome of measurement by fiat. Using paired comparisons between German parties, it can be shown that the minimal condition for rational voters—transitivity of strict preferences—is fulfilled for over 90 percent of the electorate.[11] Brady and Ansolabehere report similarly that only 2 to 10 percent of American respondents had intransitive candidate orderings over candidates in presidential primaries.[12]

In normal election studies, the data which one would need for the valid construction of utility functions over a set of parties are not available. But in many European election studies, "feeling thermometer" or "sympathy scalometer" questions are asked for all parties competing for seats in Parliament; and it is possible to exploit this type of data for a construction of the party preference profiles of voters. Before discussing different types of measurements, though, we have first to clarify the theoretical status of the concept of "party preference."

I propose to treat "party preference" as the central intervening variable between the reasoning about and evaluations of parties, on the one hand, and voting behaviour, on the other. The status of this variable is, as I have said, similar to that of "comparative candidate evaluations" in American models of the presidential vote. But to make it strictly equivalent parties would have to be presented as concrete options in the specific upcoming election. That is to say, one would have to ask voters about their party preferences concerning one specific election: for a federal election, for example, one would have to ask, "Which party do you prefer most in federal politics for the upcoming legislative period?"; and when two elections (a federal and a state election, for example) are held simultaneously, one would have to ask two election-specific party preference questions.

The alternative is to conceptualize parties as consistent players in different games and to assume that voters (especially in multi-party systems) develop general party preferences. In most democracies, the different government levels are not of equal importance, so that, empirically, parties are evaluated overwhelmingly with respect to their national role.

The degree of election- or situation-specificity is one dimension characterising party preference. A second is the time dimension. Should "party preference" just tap the momentary feelings towards parties, or should it measure a more permanent attitude? Theoretically, it seems that one's present party preference profile must be influenced by the profile of an earlier period: there has to be some continuity in these preferences. Alternatively, though, we might ask the question in a way which stresses the momentary character of preference, to the detriment of its permanent aspects. Thus on the "time" dimension, party preferences might represent either a more permanent or a more momentary attitude, just as on the first dimension party preferences might be either situation- or election-specific or not.

Party Preference and Party Identification

The concept of "party preference" is, of course, related to the concept of "party identification." In its original Michigan version, party identification is conceptualised as a permanent positive identification with a party as a general (not situation-specific) attitude object. For European multi-party systems, party identification questions have the shortcoming that a certain degree of identification with one party cannot be interpreted as the inverse of the identification with the other parties. An American-style seven-point scale (running from strong to weak Democrats through Democratic leaners and independents to strong Republicans) cannot be constructed for multi-party systems. Dutch authors have proposed an alternative measure of permanent party preference profiles which avoids concentration on the most-preferred party. The proposed question is supposed to measure general electoral utility of parties by asking respondents, for each party, how probable it is that they "will ever vote" for it.[13] Since "will ever vote" transcends the momentary aspect of preference, focusing on elections in general and not on any specific election, answers to this question can be interpreted equivalent to expressions of party identification in multi-party systems.

The more conventional "sympathy" ratings of parties stress more the momentary (though not, it is thought, election-specific) character of these attitudes. Monthly time series do show many ups and downs for the different parties. But these movements are normally not decomposed into their different components, such as the overall mean for the established parties, the variance of the respondents' ratings or the relative party ranks; and the latter may remain relatively stable, even if the mean level of sympathy or the size of the distances between parties changes. What may look on the surface like a clear candidate for a "momentary general party preference" may thus contain information on more permanent aspects of party preference, measuring an attitude somewhere in between a momentary and a permanent preference. This interpretation comes close to party identification as "a running tally of retrospective evaluations" for every party a voter perceives as relevant, where s/he continually adds positive evaluations for each party and substracts negative ones depending on experiences during legislative periods.[14]

Let us now briefly consider the other two possible conjunctions of the situation- or election-specificity and time dimensions. Pre-election polls sometimes ask situation-specific, momentary party rankings. The only combination of the two dimensions that might seem empirically empty is permanent election-specificity. But even there one can imagine voters who have different, but relatively stable, party preferences for different types or levels of elections. For example, they would never vote for a post-communist party at the national level, but they consider the respective local party as an option for a first or middle rank. Since voting research normally focuses on national elections, election-specificity is a neglected variable.

Different devices exist for assembling data on party preference profiles: paired comparisons, rankings or ratings. The latter two methods impose consistent profiles by their very design, whereas paired comparison data allow empirical tests of consistency. Conventional ranking or rating scales are frequently analysed in search of a simple spatial representation of party preference profiles. In those studies, the results of factor analysis (or of unfolding techniques applied to preference or dominance data) are interpreted as the joint decision space of the electorate, summarising the rankings or distances of the voters from the parties in the statistically best possible way. Numerous analyses of this type have been performed for multi-party systems, including Converse's early[15] study for Finland and Nannestad's sophisticated recent study for Denmark.[16] Unfolding analysis allows us to test hypotheses about the one-dimensionality of a party space. Factor analysis, in contrast, is more often applied for explanatory than for confirmatory purposes; and the interpretations of the resulting solutions do not always appear plausible, especially where more than one dimension is identified.

Preference Formation

Among the many forces affecting party preference, those singled out here are those with the most immediate impact on reasoning voters, who must make up their minds using the available political information and without investing in expensive monitoring. Citizens in modern democracies are continuously exposed to a steady flow of political information from the mass media, from discussions in their everyday lives, and so on. Not everyone is interested in politics all the time; some people may have difficulties inferring from news about domestic affairs any conclusions about the role of parties and the consequences for their party preferences. Informational short-cuts which could be relevant in this situation are: "schemata," to process and retrieve political information; "framing mechanisms" to simplify the evaluation of parties; and "retrospective evaluations" of government performance.

The concepts of schema and frame were developed by cognitive psychologists[17]and are frequently applied to voting and public opinion research.[18] Schema theory has, however, aroused controversy as a way of understanding political attitudes and behaviour.[19] The core of this controversy, as whenever a new concept is imported from one discipline into an established research field in another, is whether we gain fresh insights or whether we just retell old stories in a new jargon. Schemata—"the set of cognitions relevant to some concept"—help the individual in information processing.[20] Memory structures, and information input, processing and retrieval are modeled by psychologists for individual persons. Political psychologists, though, are more interested in convergence among citizens in their definitions of social situations; and for that task we already had concepts such as belief systems[21] and ideologies as political codes.[22]

Here, such concepts are discussed in relation to reasoning voters and their information-processing problems. Some of these older concepts were initially offered as "realist" conceptions of voters, counterposed to normative models of an informed and perfectly rational voter. What were originally conceived as deviations from *homo economicus* or from the *homo politicus* of civics textbooks can nowadays be reinterpreted as the model citizen, who uses informational short-cuts and judgmental heuristics in reasoning about politics and parties. These findings from cognitive psychology have led to new conceptualisations of rational choice which are more realistic, but which should nevertheless allow formal modeling.[23]

The minimally reasoning citizen of traditional voting research is the retrospective voter. Following the traditional reward-punishment theory of Key, retrospective voters simplify their reasoning by evaluating their own well-being in the immediate past for which they hold the incumbent government responsible, rewarding it for positive developments and blaming it for deteriorations.[24] Alternatively, retrospective evaluations right be mediated rather than direct, the citizen relying not only on his or her own experience but also on judgments of others or of the mass media about the accomplishments of the incumbent government.[25]

But what is the impact of retrospective evaluations on party preferences in multi-party systems, where coalition governments are the rule and not the exception? How citizens allocate credit for overall government achievements among parties within a coalition is essentially an empirical question. In European voting studies, questions on party competence for different policy domains are sometimes asked, and these measures can be viewed as proxies of performance evaluations. The respondents are asked to rate or rank the importance or salience of each problem, and then they are asked to name which party they think would be best in handling the issue. Even without an explicit time frame, competence evaluations seem inevitably to be based on past experiences; and in the case of elections to the European Parliament, these experiences will more likely stem from the participation of parties in national governments than in their European roles.

Simple retrospective evaluations of government performance are based on the voters' experiences and seem not to be prone to rationalisations in the way that party competence judgments often are. Even scholars relying on party competence measurements concede that these may be only reflections of more permanent affective ties to parties—that is, a consequence and not a cause of party preference.[26] The easier the evaluation task is made for respondents, the more they are tempted to report non-attitudes. This is a severe problem, especially for smaller parties, whose competence may be less visible when in government and almost impossible to evaluate when in opposition.

Rationalisation is an easy option for respondents when they are just asked to pick the most competent party, without having to compare it specifically with other parties. Sniderman *et al.* have shown that informed and less informed American voters differ in the relative importance that "incumbent approval" and "comparative prospective evaluations of candidates" have for their votes.[27] The more informed voters reason more, basing their final decision less on incumbent approval and more on a comparative candidate evaluation. They act as optimizers, whereas less informed voters just attempt "to decide whether the way things have been good enough," thereby acting as satisficers.[28] In parliamentary systems with coalition governments, satisficers are confronted with a more difficult task than in the American presidential system; but they may nevertheless choose, for example, between the larger coalition party (or the party of the prime minister) and the major opposition party. In Germany, only the Christian Democrats and the Social Democrats present candidates for the chancellorship; so that system approaches a two-party constellation, at least for the less informed who thus have a chance to avoid a complex comparison between all party options. But then it would be important to measure incumbent performance directly, instead of using questions built on the assumption that the respondents reason carefully about the comparative competence of the parties.

Party competence questions have another disadvantage as probes of factors influencing the formation of party preferences: those questions are sometimes ambiguous, in utility terms. When a respondent is asked to evaluate the competence of a party with respect to a certain policy domain such as European unification, s/he might name the party which s/he perceives as the most able promoter of unification—even though s/he is actually against further unification. A party is properly deemed "competent" if it is able to pursue its goals effectively, whether or not the respondent agrees with these goals, and a respondent who opposes further European unification can nevertheless believe that a party in favour of such a policy is very competent (and is, therefore, an able opponent of his or her own goals). Weird as this possible interpretation may look, at the very least it shows that competence questions are not a very direct way to measure the utility component of party preference. Retrospective evaluations of government performance, and judgments about future policies of the parties which a voter is able to compare with his or her own policy preferences, are much more plausible ingredients of preference formation than competence ratings.

The Voter Model

At the core of the rational voter model are the proximities of voters' "ideal points" to the perceived party positions on issue scales. Downs originally postulated that this voter will invest his or her vote in that party which promises the best returns in the next legislative period, and issue proximities are supposed to measure these prospective returns.[29] Issue positions are linearly ordered sets of policy options, resulting in a one-dimensional scale on which voters have single-peaked, symmetric preference curves. The further a voter perceives a party's position to be (in either direction) from his or her own ideal point, the greater the utility loss s/he expects if that party were to pursue its policy in government.

The reasoning voter is here assumed to differ from the original rational voter in two major respects. S/he does not form her party preferences exclusively on the basis of issue proximities, and s/he does not act as a consequential investor in that part of his or her future well-being which is influenced by government. The first aspect was already dealt with, showing how retrospective evaluations of government performance as well as issue proximities affect preference-formation.

Issue voting raises many problems for both the informed and the less informed voters. The first group is not necessarily homogeneous: these voters are not all driven by the same problems, for which they look to the government for solutions. The latter group often simply will not know which policies different parties offer as solutions. The final result could be an electorate balkanised into many issue publics, with a large rump for which issue proximities are utterly meaningless. Multi-party systems should have even more uninformed voters than two-party systems, since it is presumably more cumbersome to gather and process data on many parties than it is on only two; and assuming a proliferation of one-issue parties in such settings, balkanisation would more probably be even more characteristic of multi-party than of two-party systems.

Interestingly enough, these hypotheses are radically untrue to life in multi-party systems. A tentative explanation is given by a theory analogous to the "functional theory of party identification":[30] citizens without direct information on parties' positions concerning many issues will apply informational short-cuts; and the more they are forced to do that by features of the political system, the better oriented citizens in multi-party systems become compared to those in two-party systems.

From Downs forward, ideology has been discussed as a possible information short-cut.[31] This use of ideology should not be confused with ideological thinking in the sense of "political sophistication".[32] In that latter sense, ideologues have the highest level of political conceptualisation; they have opinions on many issues and organize their political beliefs, using abstract principles like "liberalism" or "conservativism" which are not idiosyncratic but rather which are shared by the élites; and their different attitudes are, therefore, consistent as shared "official" ideologies. The original estimate of the percentage of such ideologues in the American electorate was 2.5 percent, plus another 9 percent who where characterised as "near-ideologues".[33] Even though these numbers have increased, compared to the low levels within the American electorate in the late 1950s[34], ideological thinking has remained a minority affair and not a powerful device for "cognitive misers" in general to use in orienting themselves in the world of politics.[35]

Organising one's own attitudes in terms of "official ideologies" which function as constraints for individual belief systems is not at all necessary when citizens try to orient themselves politically with the help of ideological labels like "left" and "right." Of course, in order for them to function as orientation short-cuts at all, members of the public have to attach these labels to political parties. But even unsophisticated voters should be able to apply the left-right schema as a mere orientation device, assuming the mass media uses these labels more-or-less consistently in its discussion of political topics. Fuchs and Klingemann "view the left–right schema as a mechanism for the reduction of complexity, which serves primarily to provide an orientation function for individuals and a communication function for the political system".[36] They find that over 90 percent of the West German and Dutch electorates have at least a minimum understanding of the labels "left" and "right," whereas this figure is lower in the United States. Since the schema is closely linked in Europe to the cleavages characterising party systems, it is able to fulfill its function as an information short-cut about political contents.

Many European researchers use the left-right scale in surveys, both in order to generate data on the perceived positions of parties and to ask the respondents where they place themselves on the same scale. As a result, one has all the necessary data for a simple one-dimensional spatial model, in which differences between ideological self-placement and perceived party positions are interpreted as utility-loss terms. This is the most straightforward operationalisation of Downs's idea that many party systems are characterised by one overwhelming ideological dimension (an economic left–right scale) on which both parties and voters are located, giving general hints in a complex world about their policy preferences.

This operationalisation is appealing, since voters in European multi-party systems do indeed perceive the parties' positions on the left–right scale relatively correctly e.g., Germany[37] and Italy[38] But in order to use these data as generalised issue proximities, one has in addition to make two assumptions:

(1) the left–right dimension is the only major schema applied to parties, or at least there is not another schema which would result in a different linear order among the parties;

(2) the respondents are able to use the same orientation device about themselves as about parties, which is to say, they also perceive their own policy preferences in general left–right terms.

Hinich and his collaborators[39] have developed a theory which, instead of being built on these assumptions, actually allows an empirical test of them. One can interpret this approach as a type of schema theory, which postulates that citizens in modern democracies do indeed use ideological labels attached to parties as information short-cuts about concrete policy positions of these parties. But contrary to Downs's original model, the citizens do not have to place themselves directly on the ideological dimensions—since their primary goals are their policy preferences which can (given certain further assumptions) be summarised as derived ideological positions. Downs had originally proposed a simpler model:

> each party takes stands on many issues, and each stand can be assigned a position on our left–right scale. Then the party's net position on this scale is a weighted average of the positions of all the particular policies it upholds. Furthermore, each citizen can apply different weights to the individual policies, since each policy effects some citizens more than others.[40]

Hinich and Munger say this model does not work.[41] It cannot guarantee coherence in ideological messages, due to the different weights the voters assign to the policy positions. "If we allow for some overall coherence, we must still address the question of how voter preferences are expressed, for this expression determines which ideology parties try to associate themselves with in order to win elections." They solve this central puzzle with a new spatial theory of ideology in which "the ideological dimension(s) (where politics is debated and decided)" are related systematically "to the complex, n-dimensional policy space (which voters actually care about)."

This goal is achieved by postulating that voters have knowledge of the ideological positions of parties on one or more ideological dimensions, and that voters use that knowledge to guess about the policy stands of these parties.

Thus, one has only to assume that citizens have a vague idea of how some ideological dimension (left–right, for example) is related to policy stands (on economic redistribution, for example). Suppose a voter has the idea that leftist parties are more in favour of redistribution. From that knowledge, s/he can derive the probable positions of the parties on this policy dimension, placing parties more toward the redistributive end of the scale the more leftist they are perceived to be. But the citizen does not necessarily locate himself or herself on the left–right ideological scale: instead s/he merely has a particular preference concerning redistributive issues.

Voters may differ in their perceptions of how much the policy positions of the parties differ with respect to the basic ideological dimension. Some voters perceive rather large differences between left and right parties with respect to redistributive issues; others may think that nowadays left and right parties do not differ very much concerning such issues. Depending on these estimates, voters with the same policy preference may end up at different derived positions on the underlying ideological dimension (see Figure 1).

Where campaigns focus on a single issue, this theory would just complicate the decision situation unnecessarily. The aim of the theory is to find a few ideological dimensions consolidating several different concrete policy issues at play in campaigns or in politics more generally. Even if the number of issues is quite large, it may well be that the underlying ideological space is only one-dimensional. Still, it is an empirical question whether a party system can be characterised by only one latent ideological dimension along which the parties differ, or whether more than one latent ideological dimension underlies the political position-taking in day-to-day politics. Thus, the German liberal party is arguably perceived to occupy a middle position between the Christian Democrats and the Social Democrats only when attention is focused on law and order, abortion rights or new social issues: in economic policy terms, the same party is perceived to the right of the Christian Democrats.[42]

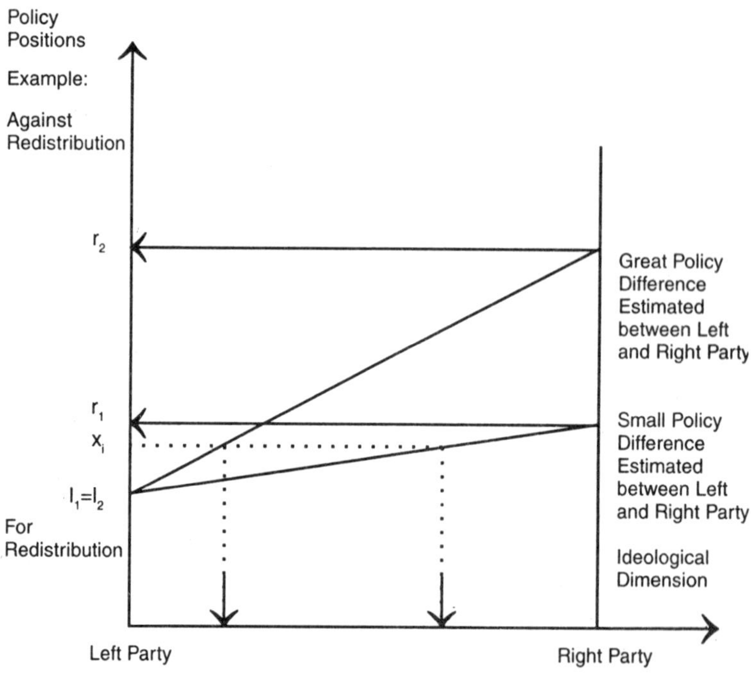

Figure 1: The policy preference of voter i (x_i) and two possible estimates of the policy positions of a left (l_1, l_2) and right party (r_1, r_2).

Empirically, there are two ways to apply Hinich's theory. One possibility is to employ data on policy preferences of voters and perceived party positions for different issues, using factor analytic methods to recover the latent ideological space.[43] The other possibility is to measure directly the ideological knowledge of the voters concerning the parties. Assuming that there is only one left–right dimension underlying policy differences in a multi-party system, one can ask the usual left–right question with respect to the parties, and then use this information as an independent variable to predict the perceived policy positions of parties on specific policy dimensions.[44] Whichever estimation method one uses, one is able to derive ideological positions for the voters which are then used as the "derived ideal points" on the so-called "predictive" dimension or dimensions. The parties have positions in the same space, so it is very easy to compute ideological distances between the voters' ideal points and the positions of the parties. These terms can then be used as independent variables, along with others, to predict people's party preferences.

Party Preferences and Voting Behaviour

On the model here in view, then, retrospective evaluations of parties and issue proximities serve, firstly as predictors of party preference formation and, secondly and through that, as predictors of voting behaviour. Clearly, "retrospective evaluations" and "issue proximities" are topics about which voters themselves reason—which is a major argument in favour of this model. But when it comes to actual voting behaviour, it is an open question of whether voters have to reason anew come every fresh election. Could not party preference or party identification of an earlier period serve as a standing decision? At least a substantial subset of voters might have finished their reasoning some time ago, and their party preferences take only the rudimentary form that they confidently know which party they like most. Then it is possible to vote in general elections just out of habit: voting being a repeated action for most voters, participation and choice could be an almost automatic consequence of a stable attitude towards one favoured party, outside the reach of conscious decision-making.[45] On the other hand, though, habits can also be seen as a conscious decision between (on the one hand) a standard option with a certain known utility and (on the other hand) an alternative with additional outcomes whose evaluation incurs additional information costs: the utility of the additional option will be expected only with a given probability, and it will not be as certain an outcome as the standard option; so the new alternative will be selected only if its expected utility is rather high, compared to the search costs.[46]

This "habit" concept is appealing, at least as applied to older cohorts with frequent experience of participating in democratic elections.[47] Some caveats should nonetheless be entered. Voting is indeed repeated behaviour, but with much longer time intervals than in everyday behaviour. Citizens are regularly confronted with news about parties but are relatively seldomly required to choose among them. In addition, voting behaviour is not costless, so that a decision to participate at all in a certain election may not be self-evident, especially when bad news about one's favourite party abounds. Reflecting upon such caveats, we can conclude that a certain amount of reasoning beyond pure habit is needed.

Whatever the forces influencing preference formation, reasoning voters summarize their impressions from party politics in a preference profile. Even pure-habit voters merely prefer their standing party to all others, and are only less open to, new party signals in the ongoing election campaign; so that their party preference of the earlier period carries over to the new election without short-term impacts. What remains to reason about are the election-specific conclusions our potential voters draw from their preferences.

Logically, the decision situation is clear enough: one has to decide whether to participate in the upcoming election, and which party to choose. In a two-party system, the most-preferred party will obviously be the party of one's choice, so the participation decision is the more difficult one. It gave rise to the voters' paradox—why vote at all, when the expected utility of one's own participation is very small or even negative, considering the participation costs. Those costs are certain, whereas the utility incomes of future governments have to be discounted by the small probability that the vote of the respective individual is decisive. Research shows that turnout at the aggregate level is positively correlated with the mean size of the party differential (utility term) and the closeness of the aggregate vote for the competing parties (probability term). Still, the overall impact of participation norms (civic duty) is very important at the individual level. Hence, many authors, even those starting from rational choice premises, end up taking participation norms as a major factor determining turnout—and as one which is independent of the instrumentally rational calculus of party choice.[48]

Those norms serve an expressive function. The satisfaction comes from the act of voting as such, not from its consequences for future governments as in the case of instrumental action. "Public choice orthodoxy seems to assume that though non-instrumental considerations are relevant in getting voters to go to the polls in the first place, such considerations cease to bear once the voter slips behind the curtain to pull a lever or mark a card".[49] Brennan and Lomasky argue that both expressive and instrumental factors play a role in party choice, as others have argued before them.[50] An example of expressive preferences are ethical principles which people uphold and see as symbolised by a party programme, without asking about the consequences of the principles in political reality. In Weberian terms, one can characterize individual voters as both instrumentally rational (*zweckrational*) and *wertrational*, that is, oriented "to an absolute value... involving a conscious belief in the absolute value of some ethical, aesthetical, religious, or other form of behaviour, entirely for its own sake and independently of any prospect of external success".[51] Since a single voter is almost never decisive in a general election, expressive considerations gain importance compared to the investment decision when a citizen invests his or her vote to maximize his or her returns from future governments.

In multi-party systems with coalition governments, citizens as investors of votes have to overcome even more obstacles than in two-party systems with alternating governments. Although having normally only the option of choosing which party to support, they are also interested in the future coalition. When the parties do not announce their coalition preferences before the election, or when election outcomes are quite uncertain, it is impossible to formulate a rational strategy aiming to secure a particular coalition government. Then voting degenerates to a reporting of first preferences. Suppose now, though, that party competition is polarised between government and opposition parties, and the government parties promise to continue their coalition: a rational voter whose most preferred party is coalition partner *A* and whose second preference is coalition partner *B* may then vote sophisticatedly, voting for *B* instead of *A* if s/he thinks s/he is more decisive for the electoral success of *B* than of *A*. But in general, we expect that voting in multi-party systems is even more characterised by expressive considerations than in two-party systems, since the complexity of the decision situation discourages prospective instrumental voting. Parties advocating this or that as an absolute value, rather than focusing on practical success-oriented politics, flourish more than in a majoritarian democracy with alternating governments. And high turnout figures seem to confirm this type of *Gesinnungsdemokratie* which often degenerates to *Stimmungsdemokratie*. In Germany, coalition majorities often depend both on the relative advantage of the largest compared to the second-largest party and on the success of the junior partner gaining more than the 5 percent threshold of valid votes. In this situation, it makes sense to choose the party whose electoral prospects are less certain, thus maximising the decisiveness of one's vote for the future preferred coalition government.[52]

Both instrumental and expressive considerations can influence the party preference formation of the reasoning voter. What is at issue is not the causes but the consequences of party preferences for actual behaviour. Is it possible to show that the voter-as-consumer draws different conclusions from his or her given party preference profile than does the voter-as-investor? The latter has to calculate his or her expected-utility streams from different future governments, whereas the former needs incentives which reward the revealing of a preference in an election.

Guttman *et al.* use the distinction between non-voting due to indifference and due to alienation to differentiate voters-as-investors and voters-as-consumers.[53] Harking back to Hotelling's original example of ice cream vendors at the seashore, they argue that "[c]onsumers abstain from buying ice cream if the closest vendor is sufficiently distant.[54] The positions of alternative vendors are irrelevant to the decision to buy ice cream [or, for voters-as-consumers, a party's programme]. Voter-investors, in contrast, are interested in the victory of the favoured party against its rival(s). Here, the difference between the positions of the favoured party and its rival(s), and not the voters political distance to his favoured party, is all-important".[55] Interpreting feeling thermometers as direct measures of utility, they construct for the American presidential election of 1976 a measure of indifference (the *difference* of those scale scores between Ford and Carter) and a measure of alienation (the *absolute level* of the preferred candidate's scale score). Analysing the University of Michigan's 1972–1976 panel, they find the absolute utility level has a statistically significant effect on the probability of voting, but the utility difference term does not. Rattinger and Krämer report similar results for Germany, where alienation is known as *Politikver-drossenheit.*[56] This sensitivity to absolute utility levels and insensitivity to utility difference suggests that voters are behaving as consumers rather than investors, and that expressive considerations are more determinative of their final act of voting.

The investor-voter in multi-party systems has to take into account the coalition possibilities, guessing probabilities of alternative coalitions on the basis of different election results. Naturally, investor-voters will reason about these possibilities during the election campaign. In between elections, however, behaviour of government officials and parties is monitored, and consequences are drawn from good and bad news and experiences, in a way which reflects upon general rather than election-specific party preference; and these alternative election-specific coalition possibilities do not loom large in investor-voters' calculations.

During that preference-formation phase, voters-as-consumers do not necessarily differ from the voter-investors. The two diverge only as the upcoming election draws closer. The consumer-voter needs more impetus from the mass media or from peers to become involved; and the more biased the information is in one direction or the other, the higher the expressive value of his or her preference revelation will be, provided that s/he agrees with the partisan flavor of this information. The voter-as-investor, in contrast, will take account of coalition expectations and may contemplate sophisticated voting; and since voting for one's second preference depends on calculations of possible aggregate results, the election laws and the different aggregation devices embodied in them may here have a direct impact on individual behaviour.

Conclusion

Continental European democracies have developed parliamentary systems in which governments are normally formed by coalitions. Two-party systems are the exceptions. The modal category is a moderate pluralism—either in Sartori's original meaning of the term of three to five parties, or with a larger number of parties which are nevertheless not sharply polarised combined with anti-system parties which gain a substantial number of votes.[57] On the one hand, these party systems make it very difficult for voters to anticipate future governments. But on the other hand, they facilitate political orientation by providing ideological signals about the positions of parties.

The reasoning voter in multi-party systems will, as I have shown, develop a "party preference profile" as a summary measure of his or her experiences and information about the performance and policy offers of the parties. Among the factors influencing preference formation are performance evaluations of governments and issue proximities. But this short list could be easily supplemented by future expectations; by competence evaluations of party leaders and candidates for government offices; and so on. These factors are substantively linked to the utility that a citizen can associate with a party as a possible provider of collective goods.

Once citizens have formed consistent preferences for the parties, the major problem is then predicting their voting behaviour, taking into account the election-specific coalition expectations as an additional factor influencing the causal path from party preference to voting behaviour. But since the single voter is not decisive, public investors differ from private investors[58] and expressive considerations gain an importance in their own right as instrumental rationality is downgraded for voters in mass electorates.[59] It is not that voters are irrational but, rather, that the voting mechanism (for instance, proportional voting in parliamentary multi-party systems) is a less-than-perfect mechanism for revealing the electorate's policy preferences.

F.U. Pappi

REFERENCES

1. A. Campbell, P.E. Converse, W.E. Miller and D.E. Stokes, *The American Voter*, New York: Wiley, 1960; *Elections and the Political Order*, New York: Wiley, 1966.
2. A. Downs, *An Economic Theory of Democracy*, New York: Harper and Row, 1957.
3. J.G. Rusk, "Issues and voting", *Research in Micropolitics, ii. Voting Behavior II*, ed. S. Long, Greenwich, Conn.: JAI Press, 1987, pp. 95–141.
4. M.P. Fiorina, *Retrospective Voting in American National Elections*, New Haven, Conn.: Yale University Press, 1981.
5. P.M. Sniderman, R.A. Brody, and P.E. Tetlock, *Reasoning and Choice*, New York: Cambridge University Press, 1991, p. 18.
6. *Ibid.*, p. 7.
7. *Ibid.*, p. 10.
8. A. Downs, *op. cit.*, 1957.
9. H. Esser (ed.), *Alltagshandeln und Verstehen*, Tübingen: Mohr (Siebeck), 1991.
10. G.B. Markus, and P.E. Converse, "A dynamic simultaneous equation model of electoral choice", *American Political Science Review*, 73, 1979, pp. 1055–70.
11. F.U. Pappi, "Die Links-Rechts-Dimension des deutschen Parteiensystems und die Parteipräferenz-Profile der Wählerschaft", *Wahlen und politisches System*, ed. M. Kaase and H.-D. Klingemann, Opladen: Westdeutscher Verlag, 1983, pp. 422–41.
12. H.E. Brady, and S. Ansolabehere, "The nature of utility functions in mass publics", *American Political Science Review*, 83, 1989, pp. 143–164.

13. C. Van Der Eijk, B. Niemöller, and J.N. Tillie, The two faces of 'future vote': voter utility and party potential, Mimeo.: University of Amsterdam, 1986.

14. M.P. Fiorina, *op. cit.*, 1981, p. 89.

15. P.E. Converse, "The problem of party distances in models of voting change", *The Electoral Process*, ed. M.K. Jennings, and H. Zeigler, Englewood Cliffs, N.J.: Prentice-Hall, 1966, pp. 175–207.

16. P. Nannestad, "Dänisches Wahlverhalten 1971–1979: Ein Modell reaktiven Wählens und einige empirische Ergebnisse", *Parteien, Parlamente und Wahlen in Skandinavien,* ed. F.U. Pappi and H. Schmitt, Frankfurt: Campus, 1994, pp. 285–306.

17. R. Hastie, "A primer of information-processing theory for the political scientist", *Political Cognition*, ed. R.R. Lau and D.O. Sears, Hillsdale, N.J.: Lawrence Erlbaum Associates, 1986, pp. 11–39; D. Kahneman, and A. Tversky, "Risiko nach Maß—Psychologie der Entscheidungspräferenzen", *Spektrum der Wissenschaft*, 5, 1982, pp. 89–98.

18. P.M. Sniderman, "The new look in public opinion research", *Political Science: The State of the Discipline II*, ed. A. Finifter, Washington, D.C: American Political Science Association, 1993, pp. 219–44; S. Iyengar, *Is Anyone Responsible? How Television Frames Political Issues,* Chicago: University of Chicago Press, 1991.

19. J.H. Kuklinski, R.C. Luskin, and J. Bolland, "Where is the schema? going beyond the "s" word in political psychology", *American Political Science Review*, 85, 1991, pp. 1341–55; M. Lodge, K.M. McGraw, P.J. Conover, S. Feldman, and A.H. Miller, "Where is the schema? Critiques", *American Political Science Review*, 85, 1991, pp. 1357–80.

20. J.H. Kuklinski, Luskin, and J. Bolland, *op. cit.*, 1991, p. 1342–55.

21. P.E. Converse, "The nature of belief systems in mass publics", *Ideology and Discontent*, ed. D.E. Apter, New York and London: The Free Press, Collier-Macmillan, 1964, pp. 206–61.

22. H.-D. Klingemann, "Measuring ideological conceptualizations", *Political Action*, ed. S.H. Barnes and M. Kaase, Beverly Hills, California: Sage, 1979, pp. 215–54.

23. S. Lindenberg, "Rationalität und Kultur, Die verhaltenstheoretische Basis des Einflusses von Kultur auf Transaktionen", *Sozialstruktur und Kultur,* ed. H. Haferkamp, Frankfurt: Suhrkamp, 1990, pp. 249–87.
24. V.O. Key, *The Responsible Electorate: Rationality in Presidential Voting 1936–1960*, New York: Vintage, 1966.
25. M.P. Fiorina, *op. cit.*, 1981.
26. M. Küechler, "Issues and voting in the European elections 1989", *European Journal of Political Research*, 19, 1991, pp. 81–103.
27. P.M. Sniderman, J.M. Glaser, and R. Griffin, "Information and electoral choice", *Information and Democratic Processes*, ed. J.A. Ferejohn and J.H. Kuklinski, Urbana: University of Illinois Press, 1990, pp. 117–35.
28. *Ibid.*, p. 131.
29. A. Downs, *op. cit.*, 1957.
30. W.P. Shively, "The development of party identification among adults: explorations of a functional model", *American Political Science Review*, 73, 1979, pp. 1039–54.
31. A. Downs, *op. cit.*, 1957.
32. P.E. Converse, *op. cit.,* 1964.
33. A. Campbell, P.E. Converse, W.E. Miller and D.E. Stokes, *The American Voter*, New York: Wiley, 1960, p. 249.
34. P.R. Abramson, *Political Attitudes in America*, San Francisco: Freeman, 1983, p. 273.
35. E.R.A.N. Smith, *The Unchanging American Voter*, Berkeley: University of California Press, 1989.
36. D. Fuchs, and H.-D. Klingemann, "The left-right scheme: theoretical framework", *Continuities in Political Actions*, ed. M. K. Jennings, J. van Deth *et al.* Berlin: Walter de Gruyter, 1990, pp. 203–34.
37. H.-D. Klingemann, "Testing the left-right continuum on a sample of German voters", *Comparative Political Studies*, 5, 1972, pp. 93–106; F.U. Pappi, *op. cit.*, 1983, p. 427.

38. G. Sani, "A test of the least distance model of voting choice", Italy, 1972, *Comparative Political Studies*, 7, 1974, pp. 193–208.
39. M.J. Hinich, and W. Pollard, "A new approach to the spatial theory of electoral competition", *American Journal of Political Science*, 25, 1981, pp. 323–41; J.M. Enelow, and M.J. Hinicm, *The Spatial Theory of Voting*, Cambridge: Cambridge University Press, 1984; M.J. Hinich, and M.C. Munger, "A spatial theory of ideology", *Journal of Theoretical Politics*, 4, 1992, pp. 5–30.
40. A. Downs, *op. cit.*, 1957, p. 132–33.
41. M.C. Munger, *op. cit.*, 1992, p. 9.
42. M. Laver, and B.W. Hunt, *Policy and Party Competition*, London: Routledge 1992; F.U. Pappi, "Parteienwettbewerb im vereinten Deutschland", *Das Superwahljahr, Deutschland vor unkalkulierbaren Regierungsmehrheiten?*, ed. W. Bürklin and D. Roth, Köln: Bund-Verlag, 1994.
43. J.M. Enelow, and M.J. Hinich, *op. cit.*, 1984, pp. 213–15.
44. M.J. Hinich, and M.C. Munger, *op. cit.*, 1992, pp. 23–25.
45. D.L. Ronis, J.F. Yates, and J.P. Kirscht, "Attitudes, decisions and habits as determinants of repeated behavior", *Attitude Structure and Function*, ed. R.P. Breckler, J. Steven and A.G. Greenwald, Hillsdale, N.J.: Lawrence Erlbaum Associates, 1989, pp. 213–40.
46. H. Esser, *op. cit.*, 1991, p. 67.
47. P.E. Converse, *The Dynamics of Party Support*, Beverly Hills, California: Sage, 1976.
48. B. Barry, *Sociologists, Economists and Democracy*, Rev edn. Chicago: University of Chicago Press, 1978.
49. G. Brennan, and L. Lomasky, *Democracy and Decision*, Cambridge: Cambridge University Press, 1993, p. 35.
50. R.E. Goodin, and K.W.S. Roberts, "The ethical voter", *American Political Science Review*, 69, 1975, pp. 926–28.
51. M. Weber, "Social action and its types", *Theories of Society*, ed. T. Parsons, *et al.*, New York: Free Press; one-volume edition, 1965, pp. 173–79.

52. G. Eckstein, *Rationale Wahl im Mehrparteiensystem, Die Bedeutung von Koalitionen im räumlichen Modell der Parteienkonkurrenz,* Frankfurt am Main: Peter Lang, 1995.
53. J.M. Guttman, N. Hilger, and Y. Schachmurove, "Voting as investment vs. voting as consumption: new evidence", *Kyklos,* 47, 1994, pp. 197–207.
54. H. Hotelling, "Stability in competition", *Economic Journal,* 39, 1929, pp. 41–57.
55. J.M. Guttman, N. Hilger, and Y. Schachmurove, *op. cit.,* 1994, p. 198.
56. H. Rattinger, and J. Krämer, "Wahlnorm und Wahlbeleiligung in der Bundesrepublik Deutschland", *Politische Vierteljahresschrift,* 36, 1995, pp. 267–85.
57. G. Sartori, *Parties and Party Systems,* Cambridge: Cambridge University Press, 1976.
58. S.L. Popkin, *The Reasoning Voter,* Chicago: University of Chicago Press, 1991, p. 10.
59. G. Brennan, and L. Lomasky, *op. cit.,* 1993.

❑❑❑

3

Institutional and Experiential Approaches

Much about political behaviour research ought simply be taken as read. The introduction of mass surveys into political science and political sociology has been an important advance. Methods for asking questions have advanced a bit, and techniques for analysing survey data have advanced a lot, in the last 30 years. Debates about the foundations of political alignment between the Columbia school, the Michigan model and exponents of "issue voting" have been valuable. The extension of survey-based studies from the U.S., first to western Europe and thence to a wide range of other countries, and some small movement towards asking internationally standardised questions, have generated additional insights. Taking all that as granted, critics still ask, "is there more to learn" about mass political behaviour?[1]

The question reflects a certain amount of disillusionment with political behaviour studies, especially with electoral analysis, as the field has developed in recent years. Once it was apparently the authentic "big science" area of the discipline, with large and capital-intensive projects, elaborate and arcane technologies of its own, and the apparent promise of knowledge-accumulation on "normal science" lines. But the pace of advance in political behaviour research has undeniably slowed in the last two decades.

Fundamental debates which 1950s and 1960s authors were confident could be sorted out by better analytic techniques, larger sample sizes, or more refined survey instruments have instead seemed more and more immune to further empirical resolution. Patterns of causation involved in political alignments remain as disputed, on theoretical and value grounds, now as ever they were—both within the field of political behaviour, and between its specialists and outsiders. As in other fields:

> Although sophisticated statistical manipulation of research data can sometimes reduce the number of causal explanations compatible with the observed correlation, ultimately the choice between them is made in the light of what seems reasonable to the researcher, perhaps in the light of other research, or in terms of the obvious temporal order among the variables.[2]

Electoral analysis in particular, relies to an extraordinary degree on the indispensable context of understanding provided by common sense in ways which often vitiate the "scientific" status of key findings.[3] For example, Nie, Verba and Petrocik carefully document a rise in issue voting among American voters in the 1970s, compared with the 1950s. But they then attribute this rise to the de-polarisation of politics in the Eisenhower years, rather than to increasing sophistication amongst voters[4]—even though they have no non-reactive measures of polarisation, relying only on impressionistic evidence for this key proposition.

The current stagnation in political behaviour research, coming after the strong hopes invested in it, in its early years, has meant an internal decline in the behavioural optimism which initially strongly informed the field and an external loss of interest in its findings. Scholars specialising in political behaviour have increasingly seemed divorced from theoretical debates elsewhere, concerned only with the routinised refinement or extension of existing work. And political scientists in other fields, such as public choice, the theory of the state, or the study of political parties and social movements, have increasingly discussed political behaviour in terms divorced from survey-based empirical enquiry—as if its limits were now seen as too constraining. I first discuss the crisis of political behaviour research as a fading of a previously strong modernist vision, and then examine some alternatives which show that there is indeed still more to learn about political behaviour.

"Modernism" in Political Behaviour Research

At first sight, the suggestion that conventional electoral studies and survey-based work on political behaviour is "modernist" may seem not very credible. Lyotard offers one of the most famous definitions of modernism, apparently light-years removed from the everyday concerns of this field:

> I will use the term modern to designate any science that legitimates itself with reference to a metadiscourse of [some] kind making explicit appeal to some grand narrative, such as the dialectics of Spirit, the hermaneutics of meaning, the emancipation of the rational or working subject, or the creation of wealth.[5]

The casual observer will find few echoes in electoral analysis of Hegelianism, Marxian historical materialism, Habermassian critique or similarly "metaphysical" ideas.

Yet postwar political behaviour research undeniably has its own grand narrative and shares many of the features which postmodernists have cited as undesirable stigmata of a modernist outlook. In this narrative the modern period is marked out as unique by the progress of democratisation, which alone provides the raw materials on which most political behaviour research is based. The whole field took off in the U.S., the earliest democracy if still one of the more equivocal ones in terms of voting participation rates.[6] And the first large-scale survey research came about at exactly the time when the stalled progress of democratisation rebounded from the low point of the early 1940s, with a huge postwar growth in the number of countries with basically free elections and the proportion of the world population living there, as shown in Table 1.

TABLE 1

The growth of liberal democracy, 1900 to 1995

	Liberal democracies		*World population*	
	States	*Population (millions)*	*Numbers (millions)*	*% living in democracies*
1900	4	130	1,608	8
1910	9	163	n.a.	n.a.
1920	18	371	1,860	20
1930	15	346	2,008	18
1940	12	217	2,294	10
1950	26	869	2,516	34
1960	32	1,169	3,019	39
1970	31	1,263	3,693	34
1980	35	1,636	4,450	37
1990	39	2,070	5,246	39
1995	40	2,263	5,765	39

Sources: Sources for the democracy figures are research by Government Research Division, London School of Economics. World population data are drawn from Borrie for 1900–40, and since 1950 from UN World Population Estimates and Projections.[7] I thank John Hobcraft of the LSE Population Studies Department for help with these data.

American pluralist political sociologists who first developed survey-based research indubitably saw democratisation as an integral element in modernisation, the rationalisation and secularisation of society, and the spread of "advanced" ideas and culture. Their missionary zeal was reflected in subtle ways in the co-operative studies which they co-authored with indigenous European scholars or those in other countries. The opening sentence of the original edition of Butler and Stokes's *Political Change in Britain* declared: "The possibility of rulers being constitutionally driven from office in a free election is relatively new in the history of government."[8] Electoral analysis was to be the unique key to the foundational processes shaping the new political age.

The key modernist feature of mainstream election studies within this implied grand narrative was its strong totalising approach. Right from the start, the Michigan school in the U.S. and in Britain attacked earlier surveys based in particular local communities, and instead espoused a single national survey inherent in which was a very high level of aggregation of de-contextualised data.[9] Their work developed large cross-sectional surveys which could normally only be carried out by a single team commanding considerable capital resources, whose controllers became powerful academic oligarchs in danger of either dominating research in a proprietorial manner or rationing access to defining survey questions to like-minded exponents of the new orthodoxy. Once a series of consistent studies had been created, and overtime panel surveys had been set up, these researchers held data sets which could be and were analysed as if they stood outside time. Many of these studies were explicitly premised on the view that the political context of the whole "modern" period has been so uniform as to render unnecessary any detailed cross-referencing between voters' responses to survey questions and their immediate political environment.[10]

The methodological assumptions underpinning this totalising approach were simple in the extreme. Central to virtually all political behaviour research, and still virtually unchallenged in 1990s studies, has been the search for *the single best decision algorithm* with which to characterize the alignments and behaviour of an entire electorate. For any analytic issue, the search is for a restricted set of variables embedded in a single equation setting out their relative influence which captures more of the variance to be explained than any other competing variables and equation. In many studies, the nominal concern with "theoretical" understanding was quickly jettisoned, and the analysis of causal pathways was relegated to the margins: instead they ran, in effect, fairly simple-minded computer-tournaments between a pool of potential independent variables, and tournaments which were only lightly refereed by the analyst at that. Electoral research thus became a contest of regression or log-linear models, each of them offering a single summation of how voters as a whole have aligned between parties or across issues. With the passage of time analysts became more skilled at analysing residuals, and searching for interaction effects between variables. But what has never been seriously disputed is that a single "comprehensive" decision algorithm should be sought, as a means of answering any outstanding question.

To make matters worse, analysts often slip into discussing voters in the archetypal singular. They do so not just in their titles—*The Changing American Voter*[11] or *How Britain Votes*[12] or *The American Voter*[13]—but also in their texts:

> The function of party identification is to enable the elector to cope with political information and to know which party to vote for.[14]

> [W]hile the social psychology of the voter may not have changed much...[15]

> [T]he emphasis is once more on... the unchanging psychology of the voter.[16]

These apparently small slips in fact betoken a deeply influential process of reification and abstraction, inherent in the whole enterprise of aggregated survey data analysis, away from the experiences and choices of actual people. A variant of this are comments in which voters as a whole are described as a single unit with anthropomorphic features. For example: "We begin... by considering whether the 1992 electorate was unusually hesitant... The idea that the electorate has grown more volatile... is often advanced".[17]

A key consequence of the totalising approach has been the construction of analyses which exclude analytically inconvenient minorities. In the early days, those were chiefly kinds of voters too few in number to fit easily into cross-tabulations, or whose incorporation would prevent the use of analytic techniques requiring a dichotomous dependent variable. Catt demonstrates that the minorities which typically "disappeared" from key pieces of analysis have included, in the U.K.: everyone in Northern Ireland, where the party system is different from mainland Britain[18]; everyone in northern Scotland, who are too expensive to poll; non-respondents to surveys; respondents who declare themselves as non-voters; and voters for all "minor" parties, such as the nationalist parties in Scotland and Wales and, for many years, even people choosing the Liberals or Liberal Democrats (who number up to a quarter of all voters since the 1980s). U.K. electoral studies represented voters as overwhelmingly concerned with the two main parties long after this had ceased to be true of real world elections. Other "minorities" were vaporised analytically by simple moves such as always referring to the archetypal singular voter as "he" and "him"; by categorising the occupational class of married women from that of their husband (creating a kind of "household" class for women only); or by not exploring clearly relevant aspects of people's social locations. Thus mainstream election studies have been constantly surprised by, and slow to respond to, the growth of politically significant cleavages and issues (for example in Britain, public–private sector conflicts, ethnicity, sexual orientation and environmental issues).

A more fundamental corollary of the monistic tendencies of mainstream voting studies has been the complete underdevelopment of techniques for exploring whether and how different groups may in fact choose how to vote using quite distinct algorithms. No proposition is more centrally denied and left unexplored than this. Very few studies have systematically tried to *simulate* voters' decisions, to define a sequence of operations and criteria which might approximate the algorithms that actual voters employ in making choices. This neglect also has consequences for the ways in which researchers interpret seemingly "obvious" data. For example, although political scientists know well enough that voters can make choices only among available options over which they have little control, Catt notes how consistently analysts slip into equating all votes received by a party as "support"—glossing the blank fact of a ballot marked in a particular way as an indication of a positive ideological or emotional response to that party, and thereby masking or denying negative voting motivations.[19] It is a small step from there to masking the doubts, cynicisms and misgivings of voters about political leaders and parties:

> "As long-established actors on the political stage *it is natural* that the parties should have become objects of mass loyalty or identification".[20]

Sheltering behind highly aggregated decontextualised data, and with a ready supply of such quick or biased deconstructions of voter behaviour to hand, electoral analysis has added disappointingly little to our knowledge of the *diversity* of ways in which people think or act politically.

It was not always so. The early 1950s survey work had a radical edge to it. In debunking the previous normatively based models of rationalistic voters, and in showing that ordinary people operated with differently structured political information from political élites, this research did not widely decode politics in left–right terms and often seemed to explain voters' alignments in line with family influences or long-term identifications with parties. Indeed, it was in this phase that voting studies seemed least modernist in their explicit repudiation of "logocentric" models and recognition of voter "irrationality." At this stage, too, studies not based on survey work still had some influence on "mainstream" thinking—such as Robert Lane's brilliant essay *Political Ideology* which intensively explored the attitudes and reactions of just fifteen individuals against their fully contextualised social backgrounds and in a manner informed by a wealth of social and political theory.

But the initial cutting edge of survey research, its disconcerting impact in shifting conventional perceptions of societal processes, has long since disappeared under accumulated layers of orthodoxy-building. Political behaviour research has progressively "rationalised" the survey-based image of voters, rebuilding *The Rational Public* in a revisionist downgrading of what stable and efficacious democratisation requires of citizens.[21] And the initial diversity of political behaviour methodologies has been replaced by a suffocating reliance on quantifiable survey data alone. Virtually all this information relies on pre-coded questions, devised by the analysts alone (rather than based on respondent's own conceptions), and often asking people to carry out completely artificial operations, such as ranking political candidates or parties on fifty-point thermometer scales simply in order to be able to use sophisticated analytic methods.[22]

The meaning of survey responses is very rarely checked against other kinds of data—there is no reinterviewing of respondents using different approaches, little cross-referencing of responses to differently phrased or slanted questions, and virtually no triangulation of quantitative and qualitative information. Single survey instruments dreamed up intuitively by analysts with a little piloting have predominated in published research, their meaning taken as unequivocal and inferred on a single "common-sense" basis.[23] The main exception, which typically takes analysts one step further from people's experiences, is the use of compound scales or indices, some pre-designed—some "emerging" iteratively as possible constructs out of the data analysis, and others computer-dredged from the response patterns by computers and rationalised *post hoc*, as with the "political principles" constructed from commercial poll data using factor analysis by Rose and McAllister.[24]

The primary internal challenge to mainstream political behaviour studies since the 1970s has come from versions of rational choice theory. But their arrival has so far posed no threat at all to the older orthodoxy's totalising approach and neglect of diversity. Originally based on a relatively complex and in principle falsifiable set of procedures, rational choice theory embodies very powerful but restrictive assumptions about actors' mind-sets, levels of information, and consistency—assumptions easily glossed in building more "realistic" applied variants. Adapted to testing within the survey methods and data analysis repertoire already developed[25], simplified rational choice approaches have increasingly emerged as an extreme form of "logocentrism"—privileging an objectified model of formal rationality and ascribing it universally to all political actors.[26] This approach too is totalising, again lending itself to phrasing in terms of an archetypal singular "voter": issue voting accounts "assume that, on each issue, the voter compares his [*sic*] own stance with that of the parties. The voter then, it is claimed, aggregates his preferences on the different issues and votes for the party which offers him, on balance, the largest number of preferred policies".[27]

From this level of discussion, it is impossible that there will emerge any empirically diversified view of the complex bases of alignments or of the multiple choice algorithms followed by citizens.

And issue voting models take further the democratisation "grand narrative" left mostly implicit in older studies. They portray an electorate once held captive by habitual or traditional family, ethnic, interest group and social class influences now (becoming) liberated by acclimatisation to liberal democracy, mass education and expanded mass media coverage to function as autonomous sources of intentionality. For example, Rose and McAllister argued that British elections had moved decisively from "closed class" to "open" competitions[28]; Sarlvik and Crewe detected a "decade of dealignment"[29] in British politics during the 1970s; and Himmelweit *et al.* claimed evidence of a new sophistication in voters' choices.[30] In all these studies modernism's teleological streak was evident. The lure of a future (imputed) destination or a detected trend led researchers to gloss present realities. Deviations, inconsistencies, backsliding and contradictions in current data are all too likely to be easily masked for analysts making such strong commitments to purposive history.

Both "issue voting" approaches and mainstream "party identification" and "political sociology" accounts agree that a fully qualitative, highly aggregate, survey data approach is the appropriate "scientific" one for political behaviour research. The primary point of mass surveys is always just to reconstruct an account of institutionally significant changes: this party's loss of support, that party's gain. Authors of both schools are aware of the restrictive limitations of survey methods, the inherent losses of understanding involved in reducing people's complex meanings to dots and dashes on computer disk. But the overwhelming response has been to carry on "perfecting" survey sampling methods, question and survey instrument design, and the methods of analysis deployed to make sense of the data.

There is now little difference between non-academic surveys (carried out for the mass media or party organisations) and the questionnaire design used by political scientists. Both political sociology and rational choice accounts in different ways have helped cement the close and symbiotic relationship which has developed between political behaviour research and practitioners of political control and manipulation technologies. In the last thirty years, as it has become professionally reputable and commercially "applicable," the subfield has increasingly restructured the electoral realities it purports to independently describe. As with virtually all other branches of professional knowledge, a key consequence of the discipline's existence has been an expansion of the technical capacity to analyze, predict and shape social behaviour—in this case, party behaviour and electoral outcomes.

Elections are now pictured by elected politicians, political party professionals, political and electoral consultants, large polling organisations, mass media commentators, advertising corporations and large numbers of voters themselves in ways which have been extensively reshaped by the mainstream and issue voting orthodoxies. The expanded "control" capability apparently conferred by political behaviour research fits closely with an "engineering" model of scientific endeavor in which truth is associated with the experimental ability to successfully manipulate social forces and predict behaviour.[31]

The potential dangers in this "industrial" application of knowledge need little elaboration.[32] The analytic neglect of minorities and concentration on quantitative modeling both find support in the adequacy of the existing tool-kit for control purposes, for successful campaigning. Political science, in this approach, is not an abstract quest for knowledge for its own sake but rather for an effective understanding of those forces (and presumptively only those forces) which structure the competition for political power.[33] In this fundamental sense most political behaviour research has been system-biased, concerned with understanding those mass political phenomena which condition the transfer or retention of institutional power, and unconcerned with phenomena which seem ineffectual under current arrangements. To pick one key example, in countries with "plurality rule" or "list"-style proportional representation electoral systems, political scientists and opinion pollsters have amassed volumes of data charting voters' first preference alignments across parties over time; but they have almost ignored the structure of voters' second or subsequent preferences, because those preferences do not immediately determine which political élite gains control of government. One hardly has to agree with Foucault that the state is "a mythical abstraction whose importance is a lot more limited than many of us think"[34] to see the limitations inherent in such a narrowly institutional approach as that.

The final modernist feature of political behaviour research has been its reliance on over-polarised antimonies and false dichotomies. It is a recurring feature of electoral studies in particular that complex theoretical positions are repeatedly expressed in a lowest-common-denominator form apparently required for empirical testing. In this distorted mirror of intellectual debate voters are either "rational" or expressive, issue attitudes are either "real" or non-attitudes, actors have "perfect" information or they do not, they operate in quite distinct "market" or "political" contexts[35], and so on. Given the defective nature of the questions asked, the inherent ambiguities of language, changes in the "framing" of questions by survey design, or external shifts in the political or policy environment, however, in many cases it is actually quite unclear how someone with a perfectly worked-out position should respond. Consider for example Heath and McDonald's panel study of some 900 British voters[36]: they argue that, between 1983 and 1987, voters in their study were more "consistent" in their party identification (itself dichotomised as "Conservatives" and "all others," although in 1983 the effective number of parties was 2.9) than in their attitude towards nationalisation-privatisation.

But suppose I favoured the privatisation of the expensive telephone system (implemented in 1983), but opposed that of the well-run gas industry (1985), and expected to make money from electricity privatisation (projected in 1987). Am I then "inconsistent"? Surely only within a very strange or limiting view of the world. At this level of aggregation, it is simply impossible for analysts to make most of their everyday judgments about how to deconstruct people's responses stick *except* by forcing them into arbitrary and artificial frameworks of their own devising. In these circumstances, it is unclear whether Schumpeter's maligning of his fellow citizens is more applicable to voters or to researchers studying them. In Schumpeter's famous phrase, "The typical citizen drops down to a lower level of mental performance as soon as he enters the political field. He argues and analyses in a way that he would readily recognize as infantile within the sphere of his real interests. He becomes a primitive again."[37]

In summary, the modernist character of political behaviour research can be detected in many places: in its implicit grand narrative of democratisation; in the strong totalising and scientistic emphasis of quantitative survey-based research; in the monism of research methods and marginalising of social minorities; in the search for a single best decision algorithm; in the "engineering" conception of knowledge, in the system-biased character of knowledge development; and in the reliance on over-polarised antinomies.

Alternatives Political Research

In the social sciences it is always easier to formulate criticisms than to find new ways of proceeding. Pragmatically, for the limitations of modernist political behaviour research to be taken seriously, it is important to show that they are correctable. If the only other option were to lapse into a vague postmodernist relativism and subjectivism, reiterating in a new guise the pre-behavioural criticisms of voting studies of the 1950s, then the *faute de mieux* option of sticking with what we have would no doubt prevail. However, as a result of the easier diffusion of processing power and the capability to store and retrieve large quantities of unstructured data, plus the accumulation of new quantitative and qualitative techniques, we seem to stand at an important turning point—a genuinely "modern" period—in the development of social science methods. The trick will be to maintain intellectual control of the new potentials. Here three avenues offer ways forward to a new style of systematic political behaviour research: methodological pluralism, disaggregating information, and a shift from an institutional to an experiential focus.

Methodological Pluralism

Methodological pluralism entails taking seriously the known limitations of pre-coded survey questions in uncovering people's complex meanings. Instead we should model political behaviour in several different ways, seeking to triangulate the perspective offered by one approach with that conveyed by others. A first step entails abandoning reliance on single survey instruments (or on more complex scales) devised by analysts in isolation, and the adoption of a more forensic survey investigation style in which alternatively worded questions on the same issue seek to uncover groups of people with distinct ways of understanding or choosing. Expensive to undertake, this approach probably implies the end of "omnibus" surveys, themselves a key support for over-totalising analytic approaches.

A next stage involves integrating survey results with other forms of quantitative information. For instance, the potential insights from cross-referencing élite-level and mass-level data within a sophisticated multi-theoretical analysis have recently been impressively demonstrated by Iversen.[38] His work builds on the theoretical space opened up by Przeworski and Sprague, who also showed how much could be derived from analysing another kind of data[39], cross-national election results.[40] To take another example, Q methodology provides a useful way of constructing ideological maps by examining how small numbers of respondents feel in detail about a large number of statements, culled from actual political discourse rather than invented by the analyst.[41] The approach could be supplemented by a more systematic way of selecting statements for inclusion, based on textual analysis of mass media databases (such as Profile or Lexis).

A further and more speculative stage would be to use the ability to search flexibly for patterns and associations in free-text databases so as to create an important supplement to mass surveys, or in the further future perhaps a replacement for them. In the 1950s, within the technology of the day, surveys seeking fixed responses to analysts' questions were the only way of gathering data systematically from a representative sample of 1,000 people in a way that could subsequently be analysed. But in the 21st century, it should be perfectly feasible to have 1,000 lightly structured and rather open-ended "conversations" between trained interviewers and respondents for a similar period of time, and to record what gets said verbatim. Storing and sifting this new kind of record using expanded information technologies, we could then analytically surface what influences people's alignments and attitudes by a process of *post-hoc* interrogation of their full text. Cross-referencing the connected texts provided by print and broadcast media databases with respondents' conversations could also begin to address the hitherto irresolvable problems of assessing the extent of citizens' autonomy and dependence in the political sphere. It should certainly allow a far more precise charting of the origins and circulation of ideas, deconstructions of meanings, and the lineages of propaganda and resistance in liberal democracies.

The current rapid growth of expertise in qualitative methods offers important additional diversity in approaches.[42] Before any mass survey finding could be taken seriously it might need to be supported by findings using other methods, such as: close textual analysis of taped interview transcripts for a subset of respondents in the main survey; a compilation of life-histories and self-completion questionnaires (possibly free-form); detailed investigation at a variety of spatial levels of how respondents' experiences were shaped; and intensive studies designed to unpick the interrelationship between direct (hence more autonomous?) experiences and mediated experiences. Ethnographic studies of particular groups, and even participant observation studies of political behaviour, have also been suggested.[43] If people's experiences can only be very partially and inadequately tapped by survey instruments, then it may simply be necessary to accept that and look for other available methods of gauging them. A loss of quantification and aggregation may well result from this switch in approach, but if so that reflects the way that people's experiences are, a situation that research must work around rather than seeking to deny.

Disaggregating Information

Disaggregating information is an important supplement to methodological pluralism. It means getting away from decontextualised and aggregated data. Instead analysts would seek to start their investigations as close as possible to the understandings of a set of people themselves, structuring research around the units and levels at which their experiences are organised. The main dimensions involved will be set by the nature of the issues being investigated, but normally they must include social locations and territorial areas.

Picturing social locations accurately depends in part on social theory, and in part on how people themselves see social arrangements. A process of iteration between theoretical work and empirical results is crucial here. Most political behaviour research classifies people in terms of conventional functional indices such as occupation, ethnicity, language-group, religion, housing, industry-type, etc. These "objective" measures need to be supplemented by other self-classifications of people. They may also involve constructing some overarching categories to capture otherwise diffused effects lost in issue-by-issue categorisations. For example, there is evidence that Americans extensively structure their thinking around what Lane terms "the market experience,"[44] learning common lessons from very diverse economic interactions which they apply across different contexts; and they perceive their interactions with government as qualitatively different in character from their private sector dealings.[45] In western Europe too, public-private sector conflicts in production and consumption contexts, have had strong implications for party competition and political behaviour.[46] Hence it may make more sense to reaggregate data around these "experienced" sectoral categories than to rely on more fragmented official classifications.

Disaggregating (and reaggregating) across geographical areas is also important National-level data provide only a summary of regional and local situations—a summary which can be misleading, especially in cross-national analyses where each country (no matter how small or large) counts for one, and none for more than one. For example, Lijphart provides an authoritative account of the effects of electoral systems.[47] Yet in his data set, countries such as Iceland and the U.S. (which is 1,000 times larger in population) feature as equivalent units; and, furthermore, the main type of data are averages of "deviation from proportionality" (DV) statistics for a given electoral system, averaged across many different elections. Probe Lijphart's figures only a little, however, and difficulties emerge. In Britain, voters in the component regions of the country *experience* levels of DV in the treatment of their choices by the electoral system that are on average one and a half times greater than the national figure, which is artificially lowered by biases towards the two main parties off-setting each other.[48] Meanwhile in Spain, people in cities and regions experience the voting system as *more* proportional than the national DV figure suggests, since the overall Spanish score reflects malapportionment effects as well as disproportionality. Here, geographical disaggregation produces a picture of the world radically different from conventional institutional accounts.

Shifting from an Institutional to an Experiential Focus

A shift from an institutional to an experiential focus entails a consistent effort to move away from system-biased ways of doing research. The concept of "experiences" as the focus of analysis may seem odd to modern eyes. From differing perspectives, both American pragmatists such as John Dewey and the British conservative philosopher[49] Michael Oakeshott emphasized the grounded and contextualised quality of experiences, and the ways in which they accumulate into intuitions (which Dewey called "funded experiences").[50] These earlier insights were marginalised by postwar behavioural research, however. In studies of political behaviour the orthodox assumptions have been that people formulate attitudes (in mainstream accounts) or preferences (in issue-voting models), which they subjectively recognize and then directly display in actions. This stance ignores the many ways in which situational constraints (such as interaction and interdependency effects) can prevent attitudes or preferences being expressed in behaviour, and perhaps even recognised.[51]

Scurrying across the complexities and contextualisation of people's experiences can also lead analysts to draw conclusions which are unwarranted. Take a simple example: accounts of national elections generally assume that the alignments being charted are formulated in relation to that specific election. In fact, people might quite rationally choose whom to vote for on the basis of the overall success of that alignment across a variety of elections—after all, most countries have at a minimum national, state or regional, constituency) and local elections.[52] Again, collecting information on how many preferences people have across parties, and how positive or negative these evaluations are, may be critical for understanding in an academic (as opposed to a "control") sense the mainsprings of alignments or political attitudes. Even when we move on to supposedly "objective" data, such as that derived from electoral outcomes, the distinction between an institutional and an experiential approach remains important. The institutional way of calculating DV, for example, captures part of the picture—the ways in which electoral systems condition the transfer of seats (and hence access to state power) between political parties.[53] But it neglects the equally important question of how voting systems condition people's experiences of voting, by either recognising or ignoring their choices.[54]

An experiential approach is also preferable because political science does not have a very good record in anticipating what will or will not prove to be institutionally important. Major political change almost invariably takes the form of previously "peripheral" or marginal phenomena suddenly assuming core importance, or growing steadily in overall influence despite a string of specific defeats. Most key social movements—the women's movement, civil rights in the U.S., environmentalism in the early 1970s and later

1980s, sexual politics, and contemporary far-right politics—have emerged into prominence largely unheralded by political behaviour research focusing myopically only on those things which are already institutionally significant.

The *gestalt* shift entailed in moving from institutional to experiential measures is a subtle one. Its key element is a determination to map and chart those interactions, processes and linkages experienced as important by citizens themselves, whether or not they issue in immediately efficacious political consequences. Existing totalising approaches have reached a plateau in their ability to explain. A more differentiated approach could help to illuminate why under one set of conditions diverse choice algorithms result in a given aggregate outcome, when a relatively small change of conditions can produce different overall results.

Conclusion

In political behaviour research, as in other areas of modern thought, "we have paid a high enough price for the nostalgia of the whole and the one"[55], and suffered enough in intellectual self understanding from "the coercion of a formal, unitary and scientific discourse".[56] It does not follow, however, that we should simply lapse into relativistic critique, as postmodern theory in general might be taken to recommend. In other areas—such as architecture, planning, literature, and various parts of the social sciences—postmodernist criticisms have been taken on board as part of an overall process of constructive disciplinary self-renewal, resulting in significant changes of approach. For political behaviour research the same potential now exists. And the diminishing returns to effort from existing approaches suggest that the painful costs of adjustment might be more easily borne.

P. Dunleavy

REFERENCES

1. P. Dunleavy, "Mass political behavior, is there more to learn?", *Political Studies*, 38, 1989, pp. 453–69.

2. P. Halfpenny, *Principles of Method*, London: Longman, 1984, p. 4.

3. C.E. Lindblom, and D. Cohen, *Useable Knowledge*, New Haven, Conn.: Yale University Press, 1979, p. 17.

4. N.S. Nie, S. Verba, and J. Petrocik, *The Changing American Voter*, Cambridge, Mass: Harvard University Press, 1979, p. 192.

5. J.-F. Lyotard, *The Postmodern Condition*, Minneapolis: University of Minnesota Press, 1984, p. xxiii.

6. T. Vanhanen, *The Emergence of Democracy: A Comparative Study of 119 States, 1850–1979*, Helsinki: Societas Scientiarum Fennica, 1984, p. 115.

7. W.D. Borrie, *The Growth and Control of World Population*, London: Weidenfeld and Nicholson, 1970, p. 6.

8. D. Butler, and D. Stokes, *Political Change in Britain*, 2nd edn. London: Macmillan, 1969/1974, p. 15.

9. A. Campbell, P. Converse, W.E. Miller, and D. Stokes, *The American Voter*, New York: Wiley, 1960; D. Butler, and D. Stokes, *op. cit.*, 1969/1974.

10. A. Heath, G. Evans, J. Field, and S. Witherspoon, *Understanding Political Change: The British Voter, 1964–87*, Oxford: Pergamon, 1991.

11. N.S. Nie, S. Verba, and J. Petrocik, *op. cit.*, 1979.

12. A. Heath, R. Jowell, and J. Curtice, *How Britain Votes*, Oxford: Pergamon, 1985.

13. A. Campbell, P. Converse, W.E. Miller, and D. Stokes, *op. cit.*, 1960.

14. M. Harrop, and W.L. Miller, *Elections and Voters*, Basingstoke: Macmillan, 1987, p. 134.

15. A. Heath, G. Evans, J. Field, and S. Witherspoon, *op. cit.*, 1991, p. 200.

16. I. Crewe, and P. Norris, "In defence of British election studies", *British Elections and Parties Yearbook 1991*, ed. I. Crewe, P. Norris, D. Denver and D. Broughton. Hemel Hempsted: Harvester-Wheatsheaf, 1992, p. 19.
17. P. Clifford, and A. Heath, "The election campaign", *Heath, Jowell and Curtice 1994*, 1994, p. 6.
18. H. Catt, What Do Voters Decide? Tactical Voting in British Politics, Ph.D. dissertation, Department of Government, London School of Economics and Political Science, 1996.
19. *Ibid.*, 1989.
20. D. Butler, and D. Stokes, *op. cit.*, 1969/1974, p. 34.
21. B.I. Page, and R.Y. Schapiro, *The Rational Public: Fifty Years of Trends in Americans' Policy Preferences*, Chicago: University of Chicago Press, 1992.
22. B.I. Page, and B. Jones, "Reciprocal effects of policy preferences, party loyalties, and the vote", *American Political Science Review*, 73, 1979, pp. 1071–89.
23. G. Bishop, J. Tuchfarber, and R. Oldendick, "The nagging question of question wording", *American Journal of Political Science*, 22, 1978, pp. 250–69; J.L. Sullivan, J. Piereson, and G. Marcus, "Ideological constraint in the mass public: a methodological critique and some new findings", *American Journal of Political Science*, 22, 1978, pp. 233–49.
24. R. Rose, and I. McAllister, *Voters Begin to Choose: From Closed Class to Open Elections in Britain*, London: Sage, 1986.
25. M. Fiorina, *Retrospective Voting in American National Elections*, New Haven, Conn.: Yale University Press, 1981.
26. M.J. Hinich, and M.C. Munger, *Ideology and the Theory of Political Choice*, Ann Arbor: University of Michigan Press, 1994.
27. A. Heath, and S. McDonald, "The demise of party identification theory?" *Electoral Studies*, 7, 1988, p. 96.
28. R. Rose, and I. McAllister, *op. cit.*, 1986.

29. B. Sarlvik, and I. Crewe, *Decade of Dealignment,* Cambridge: Cambridge University Press, 1983.
30. H.T. Himmelweit, P. Humphreys, M. Jaeger, and M. Katz, *How Voters Decide*, New York: Academic Press, 1985.
31. M. Camhis, *Planning Theory and Philosophy*, London: Tavistock, 1979.
32. M. Foucault, *Power/Knowledge*, trans. and ed. C. Gordon, New York: Pantheon, 1980.
33. A. Heath, B. Taylor (eds.), *Labour's Last Chance? The 1992 Election and Beyond*, Oxford: Pergamon, 1994.
34. J. Hoffman, *Beyond the State*, Oxford: Polity, 1995, p. 162.
35. G. Brennan, and L. Lomasky. *Democracy and Decision*, Cambridge: Cambridge University Press, 1993.
36. A. Heath, and S. McDonald, *op. cit.,* 1988.
37. J. Schumpeter, *Capitalism, Socialism and Democracy*, 6th edn. London: Counterpoint; originally published 1943; rpt. 1987, p. 262.
38. T. Iversen, "The logic of electoral politics: spatial, directional and mobilizational effects", *Comparative Political Studies*, 27, 1994, pp. 155–89.
39. A. Przeworski, and J. Sprague, *Paper Stones: A History of Electoral Socialism*, Chicago: University of Chicago Press, 1986.
40. P. Dunleavy, *Democracy, Bureaucracy and Public Choice*, Hemel Hemsptead: Harvester-Wheatsheaf, 1991, Chaps. 4 and 5.
41. J.S. Dryzek and J. Berejekian, "Reconstructive democratic theory", *American Political Science Review*, 87, 1993, pp. 48–60; J.S. Dryzek, "Australian discourses of democracy", *Australian Journal of Politics*, 29/2, 1994, pp. 221–39.
42. F. Devine, "Learning more about political behavior: beyond Dunleavy", *British Elections and Parties Yearbook 1994*, ed. D. Broughton *et al.* London: Frank Cass, 1994, pp. 215–28.
43. *Ibid.*
44. R.E. Lane, *The Market Experience*, Cambridge: Cambridge University Press, 1991.

45. R.E. Lane, "Procedural goods in a democracy: how one is treated versus what one gets", *Social Justice Research*, 2, 1983, pp. 177–92; "Market justice, political justice", *American Political Science Review*, 80, 1986, pp. 383–402.

46. P. Dunleavy, "The growth of sectoral cleavages and the stabilization of state expenditures", *Environment and Planning D: Society and Space*, 4, 1986, pp. 129–44.

47. A. Lijphart, *Electoral Systems and Party Systems*, Oxford: Oxford University Press, 1994.

48. P. Dunleavy, and H. Margetts, Disaggregating Indices of Democracy: Deviation from Proportionality and Relative Reduction in Parties. Paper to Workshop on "Measuring Democracy," the European Consortium for Political Research Joint Sessions, University of Leiden, 11–17 April 1993.

49. J. Dewey, *Human Nature and Conduct*, New York: Henry Holt, 1922.

50. M. Oakeshott, *Experience and Its Modes*, Cambridge: Cambridge University Press, 1933.

51. K. Dowding, *Political Power and Rational Choice*, Aldershot, Hants.: Edward Elgar, 1991.

52. P. Dunleavy, and H. Margetts, "The rational basis for belief in the democratic myth", *Preferences, Institutions and Rational Choice*, ed. K. Dowding and D. King, Oxford: Oxford University Press, 1995, pp. 60–88.

53. R. Taagepera, and M.S. Shugart, *Seats and Votes*, New Haven, Conn.: Yale University Press, 1989, pp. 104–11.

54. P. Dunleavy and H. Margetts, "Auditing democracy: the case for an experiential approach", *Defining and Measuring Democracy*, ed. D. Beetham, London: Sage, 1994, pp. 155–81.

55. J.-F. Lyotard, *The Postmodern Condition*, Minneapolis: University of Minnesota Press, 1984, p. 81.

56. M. Foucault, *op. cit.*, 1980, p. 85.

❑❑❑

4

Tradition and Transformation

A historical review of political behaviour in the United States should really encompass at least three epochs, the new, the old and the very old. As a member of the research community for almost fifty years, it seems appropriate for me to comment briefly on the old and the new, but I will leave the tracing of the longer lines of intellectual origin to the sociologists of knowledge and the philosophers of science. If one, therefore, bypasses the early work of Stuart Rice, Samuel P. Hayes, Jr., or better known figures[1] such as Merriam and Gosnell, the era of the "Old" must be introduced with Lazarsfeld and Berelson.[2] The Huckfeldt—Carmines chapter provides a good statement on their work, as well as that of our role model in political science, V. O. Key, Jr. The only major omission from their review of the literature are the contributions provided by Stein Rokkan, including his well-known collaboration with Lipset. Rokkan, along with Lazarsfeld, saw politics and mass political behaviour as manifestations of social structure and social experience. Against that Old World backdrop, the introduction of a micro-analytic social psychological perspective was more dramatic than many retrospective accounts reveal.

For many of us in the next generation, the world of political behaviour was introduced in 1952 with the first national election study carried out by the Political Behaviour Programme of the University of Michigan's Survey Research Center. The 1952 study did not spring full-blown from imaginative minds (or deep pockets) at the University of Michigan. Under the leadership of Pendelton Herring, then President of the Social Science Research Council, the Council Committee on Political Behaviour had been formed in 1949 and was, in fact, the sponsor of the 1952 study. In the same period the Ford Foundation created the Center for Advanced Study in the Behavioural Sciences in Palo Alto, symbolising the emergence of the behavioural emphasis in the social sciences. Political behaviour in general, and electoral behaviour in particular, owes much to the private foundations, including Rockefeller, Carnegie, Russell Sage and Markle. These organisations provided a context of enthusiasm, as well as funding, throughout the decades of the 1950s and 1960s. The Ford Foundation, through the efforts of Foundation officers such as Peter de Janosi and Kalvin Silvert supported research activities and the development of institutional infrastructures associated with pioneering work in political behaviour at numerous sites in South America as well as Europe. The National Opinion Research Center at Chicago and the Institute for Social Research at Michigan were new institutional homes for behavioural research.

The Behavioural Approach to Political Science

Organised support for the behavioural approach to Political Science was centered in the SSRC, but the American Political Science Association provided disciplinary legitimacy, in part through the leadership provided by Evron Kirkpatrick, Executive Director of the then recently established Washington office. As one example, Kirkpatrick was directly responsible for the recognition of Political Science by the National Science Foundation. Kirkpatrick and others in the APSA leadership also were involved in making the International Political Science Association a supporting mechanism for cross-national collaboration. IPSA recognised "work groups" that provided legitimising umbrellas covering like-minded research scholars whose research projects would often turn to UNESCO for institutional support.

It is useful to begin this essay with the many references to institutional support for political behaviour in order to make the point that there were many new, highly relevant, organisational initiatives outside the halls of the academy proper. In their newness, the leaders of the initiatives conveyed a shared sense of optimism and challenge that encouraged members of the political science research community to explore new work ways. It also, unhappily, permits one to contrast the "Old" with its many sources of funding support with the "New," in which NSF has, by default, come close to the role of sole source supplier in the United States. However, to my mind, the contrast is less well defined by the resulting levels of financial support than by the diversity of organisations outside of government and academe that were ready to help those who saw in the new methods of data collection and data analysis the means of doing innovative research on traditional intellectual problems of the disciplines.

Which is not to say there was no institutional resistance in the halcyon days of the 1950s and 1960s. For too long the norm across political science departments in the United States was for each department to have one political behaviourist in captivity—one, but usually no more. Even at Michigan, the late George Belknap—a co-author with Angus Campbell of the pioneer article on Party Identification (and a University of Chicago Ph.D. under Avery Leiserson, a member of the SSRC Political Behaviour

Committee) was not accepted as a member of the department, and Samuel J. Eldersveld was the lone representative of the behavioural persuasion in the Michigan department until the late 1950s. Indeed, the era began with some likelihood that political behaviour would become political sociology as it was on the eastern side of the Atlantic. Illustratively, James C. Davies, one of the colleagues working on the 1952 study, joined the American Psychological Association because of a fear that political science would never accept the social psychological perspective being emphasised at Michigan.

Multi-disciplinary Origins

Put more positively, political behaviour had its origins in the multidisciplinary world of post-World War II social science. For example, the leader of the quadrumvirate responsible for *The American Voter*[3], Angus Campbell, was trained as an experimental psychologist at Stanford and was one of the pre-World War II initiators of social psychology as an academic discipline. The second in the alphabet of authors, Philip Converse, was an early product of the University of Michigan's post-World War II doctoral programme in social psychology who brought a degree in sociology to his emerging specialisations (after a baccalaureate in English literature). As the third of the group, I was a mutant political scientist whose academic work as a doctoral student in social science at Syracuse University consisted of one course in international relations and three sequences of course work in the methodologies and research methods of anthropology, sociology and social psychology. Donald Stokes was the only one with professional training as a political scientist out of Princeton and Yale; and even he came to Michigan on a pre-doctoral fellowship to study mathematical statistics in an era in which the slide rule and McBee sort cards were only slowly giving way to Hollerith cards and analog computers.

In the 1950s Michigan was joined by Yale University and the University of North Carolina as pre-eminent centers for the study of political behaviour. In the case of UNC, the disciplinary environment was similar to Michigan in that sociology, anthropology and social psychology were companion disciplines to political science, and research scholars benefitted from the UNC Institute for Social Research—a parallel to the Michigan ISR. The North Carolina focus in political behaviour was somewhat more sociological than at Michigan, and their signal contribution, among many noteworthy works, was the Prothro and Matthews study, *Negroes and the New Southern Politics.*[4] The fieldwork was done by the Michigan Survey Research Center and the study design included four intensive community studies purposively selected from the primary sampling units that were the basis for their cross-sectional study of voting behaviour in the South.

The most celebrated of the community studies of political behaviour was directed by Robert Dahl at Yale (another member of the SSRC Political Behaviour Committee) and published as *Who Governs: Democracy and Power in an American City* (1961). It complemented other political behaviour research of the day as empirical work of a behavioural orientation clearly prompted by questions of primary concern to political science.

In 1962 the Michigan SRC carried out the fieldwork for a study of public attitudes toward and understanding of the United States Supreme Court. The principal investigators were Joseph Tanenhaus, Professor of Political Science at the University of Iowa, and Walter Murphy, Professor of Politics at Princeton. Their data collection reflected the excitement created in different corners of the discipline by the capacity to use the new methods and techniques of social science to create data tailored to the research needs of the research scholar. The generic contrast, to be found in sociology as well as political science, lay in the many differences between data collected in the course of society's social book-keeping for administrative or bureaucratic purposes (birth rates, divorce rates, election statistics) and data collected expressly for use in social research.

It is true that *The American Voter*, as the successor to *The Voter Decides* with its early emphasis on predispositions (party, candidate, and issue orientations), made heavy use of attitudes and beliefs in attempting to understand individual level vote decisions.[5] And the psychological nature of party identification apparently imprinted the emphasis on social psychology as the hallmark of the Michigan school. It should be noted, however, that politically relevant relationships between the individual citizen and the social group—both primary and secondary—were major themes in the Michigan data collections of 1952 and 1956, well beyond the innovative measurement of party identification. And, indeed, at least seven chapters in *The American Voter* were given over to "sociological" concerns.

It is pertinent to note how many of the themes introduced by Huckfeldt and Carmines under the heading of political sociology's challenge were, by yesterday's lights, in the same intellectual mode as *The American Voter*. At least in part because Ted Newcomb of Bennington Study fame was a prominent part of our social and intellectual environment, we started planning for what has become the flagship of studies of political socialisation hard on the heels of the completion of *The American Voter*. The initial planning and negotiating with the Danforth Foundation, the ultimate funding source for the first 1965 data collections under the direction of Kent Jennings, were prompted by our shared conviction that crucial values and beliefs of voters are first formed in pre-adult years, and the contributions of family, school and peers to that formation should be systematically studied. The idea that there was something essentially sociological and therefore "different" about our projected panel study of political socialisation and maturation did not occur to us. The urgency of the need to expand the age range coverage of our subjects and the need to introduce diachronic variations in their experience into our research design seemed obvious and completely in the intellectual mode of *The American Voter*. In like manner the data skillfully analysed in Finifter's study of politics and the workplace (1974) were collected by Miller and Stokes in 1961 as that year's Detroit Area Study.[6] To be sure, the Detroit Area Study was a research vehicle maintained by the Department of Sociology at Michigan but, as with the Jennings socialisation study, being in Michigan made the workplace study seem a natural outgrowth of analyses pursued in Section IV (chaps. 12–18) of *The American Voter*.

Political Science was the intellectual and disciplinary home for the Miller—Stokes study of Representation in Congress. That study joined a growing list of innovative uses of new methodologies to investigate age-old questions of political behaviour. The Wahlke-Eulau study of state legislators, published as *The Legislative System*,[7] had begun in 1955 (again with the sponsorship of the SSRC Committee on Political Behaviour) and demonstrated the feasibility of carrying out systematic data collection from political élites. This capacity was exercised again by Eulau a decade later as he and Prewitt published *Labyrinths of Democracy: Adaptations, Linkages, Representations, and Policies in Urban Politics*.[8]

In 1974, near the end of the "Old" period, three closely interrelated studies were promoted by the Michigan Center for Political Studies. With support from the National Science Foundation and Russell Sage, the 1974 elections were the center of attention for interrelated studies of (1) the voters (2) the campaigns for election to the U.S. House of Representatives as reported by a national sample of candidates and campaign managers in contested races and (3) the media presentation to the voters of those campaigns. Some of the research of Erbring and MacKuen reported by Huckfeldt and Carmines exploited the data from that 1974 effort. Studies of campaign strategies as planned by campaign managers, as reported by editors and political reporters, and as viewed by voters had been synchronised because of the obvious functional interdependence of the three sets of actors. Incidentally, the three element design, this time centered in elections to the United States Senate, is currently being replicated by two of my Colleagues, Professors Kim Kahn and Patrick Kenney at Arizona State University. Both are Political Scientists and both are well trained in behavioural research approaches and methods that originated in a wide array of social science disciplines.

The list could be extended, but the point is not so much to review the research programme originating with the Michigan Center for Political Studies as to illustrate how many different studies were seen by their principal investigators as tightly interconnected parts of a substantive, coherent whole that only coincidentally embraced components that might be identified with different disciplines and were made possible by a thoroughly interdisciplinary set of research methods and techniques. Each study was shaped by principal investigators with somewhat different combinations of interests and skills and varied disciplinary training but with virtually no self-conscious interest in being "interdisciplinary." The strengths of the studies depended on borrowing concepts, hypotheses and research methods and techniques from each of several academic disciplines and applying them as the internal logic of each component of an overall research design took shape. It may be useful to sort out the various disciplinary contributions—or origins—of "New" research on political behaviour. Among the "Old" studies the interdisciplinary mix of insights and skills seemed thoroughly natural.

New Aspects of Political Behaviour Research

The Old and the New differ in at least three respects. In part because so many of the "Old" data collections were simple cross-section snapshots of a large and complex set of "variables" derived from large and heterogeneous populations, methodological creativity was called upon to overcome limitations inherent in the data. Inadequacies were particularly obvious in data intended to represent a "process" such as involved in voters arriving at vote choices. This need for methodologies to overcome deficiencies in the data was complemented by an inventiveness that was soon its own spur, speeding new developments as courses on "research methods" proliferated and "political methodology" became the focus for professional organisational activity.

For whatever reasons, analytic sophistication, or complexity, now seems to be of the essence in much newly published work. The propensity to begin data analysis with simple bivariate or trivariate inquiries has disappeared in order to hasten on to "model" a new idea with many-termed multi-variate equations. Whether this, in general, is a mark of the superiority of the "New" over the Old is a matter for another set of chapters. It would appear, however, that being up-to-date in Method City is at least as important as testing a new substantive idea or theoretical insight. As a consequence, "New" research is less often inspired by the prospect of a new venture into heretofore unchartered domains of politics and government and more often a trek through essentially familiar terrain in a new analytic vehicle.

The evolution of new analytic perspectives and techniques has, of course, been made possible largely through the agency of the computer, a second source of transformations from the "Old" to the "New." As the data were collected for Almond and Verba's *Civic Culture*, Dahl's *Who Governs*, or *The American Voter*, data processing and analytic calculations were accomplished with the eighty-column Hollerith (IBM) card and mechanical card sorting devices—the counter sorter or the "101" with its complex wiring boards to produce more complex counting and sorting. The original data for the Elmira Study underlying Lazarsfeld and Berelson's seminal volume, *Voting*[9], are still carried in the ICPSR archives on multiply-punched cards—with two variables often encoded in a single column dividing the twelve rows between them. Analyses for *The Voter Decides* were based on "analysis cards," in which a sub-set of variables pertinent to a single piece of analysis had been transferred from their original storage cards and brought together so they were physically located on the same analysis card.

Although this cumbersome technology was a vast improvement over hand recording on tabulating paper, it placed a high premium on data management, and documentation tailored to fit each stage, and it placed severe limits on the complexity of analytic techniques that could be used. The computer changed—and is still changing—all of that. All twenty-three studies in the American NES forty years series are now available, with complete detailed documentation, on a single compact disc that also carries front-end software to facilitate access to the data. The capacity of computer software for multivariate analyses will today accommodate data sets ranging across scores of variables for thousands of cases. These storage, retrieval and processing capabilities have encouraged the proliferation of both methodological and substantive interests and have made possible research that could scarcely have been imagined forty years ago.

The third crucial change that has occurred over the past thirty years has been in the social organisation of access to data. The first years of the behavioural revolution were marked by a veritable explosion of empirical studies based on data collected from large and politically significant populations. In electoral behaviour, there were studies of national electorates, and in legislative behaviour, studies of second chambers in national governments. However, by virtue of traditional academic culture, and in the absence of any alternative, exploitation of each new data collection in the 1950s was largely restricted to the principal investigators and their graduate students.

In an effort to expand the numbers of scholars who could have access to the 1952 and 1956 Michigan election studies, the same SSRC Political Behaviour Committee so essential to the funding of those studies sponsored and underwrote two summer training seminars at the Michigan Survey Research Center in 1954 and 1958. Participants included such latent luminaries as Robert Lane and Heinz Eulau. Converse, Miller, and Stokes were the instructors and each summer was devoted to teaching about and learning about codebooks and crosstabs and computation of Chi squares. The summers were exciting, new experiences in collegial learning and doing, and new experiences in the world of data processing.

The 1954 experience inspired Eulau to return to Ann Arbor in 1955 and launch his work on politics and social class. The modal sequel to the seminars was less rewarding. Scholars returned to their departments with a new awareness of the absence of the infrastructure necessary to extend or continue the Michigan experience. And this even in many of the best departments of political science. Out of an awareness of the difficulty experienced by most seminarians who wanted to continue their new work ways at home, the idea of the Inter-University Consortium for Political Research was born.

The idea had two components. The first was to establish the cultural norm of sharing data. The traditional norm gave to the creator or generator of data a virtually proprietary right to control access to the data. The new concept emphasised sharing data resources, particularly if they were initially created through public funding. The other principal component of the original idea of the Consortium was the goal of creating a new organisation to facilitate individual research efforts, but to be supported by departments of political science. It would maintain data libraries (unfortunately improperly labelled "archives"), built on data contributed by principal investigators to be shared with colleagues. The organisation would also provide the training needed for access to the data and for facilitating data analysis. It would provide the infrastructure needed for the exploitation of extensive data resources to be shared by individual research scholars otherwise separated from each other.

Today ICPR has become ICPSR, and through the early leadership of people such as Jean Blondel, Stein Rokkan, Erwin Scheuch and Rudolf Wildenmann there is a thriving ECPR. Bergen, Cologne, Essex, and others have established data archives that complement the largest of the data collections maintained in Ann Arbor by the ICPSR.

Most recently, yet another organisational innovation has appeared to promote the "Comparative Study of Electoral Systems." With the leadership of John Curtice from England, Sören Holmberg from Sweden, Hans-Dieter Klingemann from Germany, Steven Rosenstone from the United States and Jacques Thomassen from the Netherlands, plans are underway to make national election studies, around the world, vehicles for systematic cross-national comparative studies. The focus is sharply on electoral behaviour, but the micro-analysis of individual behaviour in each country will be enhanced with data on the contexts provided by social and economic factors relevant to each country.

The Impact of the New on the Old

The ultimate consequences of the revolutions in methods, computer applications and human organisation cannot be anticipated in any detail. There will certainly be an extraordinary increase in the sheer volume of research. Technical standards will almost certainly go up on all fronts—data collection, data analysis and theoretical explanations of political behaviour in varied settings. However, given cultural and linguistic differences across communities of scholars, it is also likely that research technology will continue to outpace and overwhelm substantive discovery.

On the other hand, concerns such as those expressed in the previous chapter are not simply methodological concerns, and they are slowly being addressed, or redressed. The work of Huckfeldt and Sprague, among others, certainly speaks directly to the need for disaggregation and reaggregation at the level of individual experience. Among the "older" works that attended to similar concerns involving a quite different topic is the Verba–Nie volume on political participation. In general, I think it is as easy to underestimate the very real concerns of "Old" behavioural researchers over questions of heterogeneity among their respondents as it is to underestimate the cost of doing something about it. At the same time, it may be that there is a real problem in overestimating the extent or the consequence of experientially based heterogeneity. At least in the domain of trying to explain an elector's vote choices, the search for evidence that voters coming from different circumstances use different paradigms in their decision-making has not been rewarding. Noting that virtually every summary measure of a relationship represents some "average" among voters, including many for whom the summary is just not appropriate, is well and good—but what to do? I do not think the fault lies in a preoccupation with institutional definitions of meaningfulness so much as with the inadequacy of resources with which to design proper data collections. The "Old" did not do well in this domain, but not because the problems were not recognised.

Franz Pappi's concern is, in my view, another version of the Dunleavy concern. The particular application to the multi-party election has not drawn enough attention in the United States largely because it is so seldom that American voters have a real opportunity for strategic voting in Presidential elections. It is possible that a repetition of 1992 would change all of that. The chapter by Pappi is crucially important because it complements the other preoccupations with American politics and American political science with a major contribution from European political culture. In particular, it brings the consideration of coalition formation into the analytic calculus.

On this score I can only say, tell us more. Most American analysts do not cope well when the voter has more than two alternatives. A third candidate is either ignored, as were Wallace in 1968 and Anderson in 1980, or given separate treatment, as with Perot in 1992. The notion that some voters may have a calculus based on strategic voting is often enunciated but seldom examined. At the same time, I would note the possibility of utilising candidate "thermometer" data as an alternative to many examples of modeling rational choice theories. The problem can at least be reduced if analyses seek to adopt the voter's perspective and are, therefore, limited to the apparent contest, voter-by-voter, between the two most favoured candidates. In 1992, analyses eliminating less preferred candidates provided persuasive explanations of the Perot vote without invoking concepts of strategic voting.[10]

New Definitions of Citizenship

In as much as each line of inquiry into mass electoral behaviour develops its own empirical generalisations united by their own logic, and progresses by the constant interplay of theory and evidence, it would take the unseen guiding hand of an Abigail Smith to produce a new empirical model of the democratic citizen. It seems to me that we are not in the process of developing a new model of the democratic citizen so much as we are learning about the conditions and circumstances under which varied and different categories of citizens respond politically in understandable and understandably different ways. Although much political philosophy and much élite political behaviour rests on one or another conception of the average or typical or modal member of the rank and file citizenry, much of the research on large populations, such as national electorates, documents the heterogeneity of responses to common stimuli.

More generally, it seems to me that the challenge of democratic theory has, indeed, supplied "much of the agenda for political behaviour research during the past 50 years," but only in the broadest sense. It is true that the felt need to understand better the voting behaviour of an entire electorate is drawn from the conviction that elections are vital institutions in democratic politics. Much work on specific topics is on the agenda by virtue of institutional definitions of a problem. It is also true that *after the fact* there is often speculation about the meaning which a newly verified generalisation has for this or that aspect of normative philosophy. However, it is also true that verification of empirical generalisations is seldom sought because of their potential implication for theories of democratic governance. Generalisations are usually re-examined because verification, or rejection, has implications for our theories about the causes of a given behaviour.

What we have learned about mass electoral behaviour certainly has meaning for theories of democratic politics. But as yet we are often uncertain as to what the various meanings ultimately will be. It may be that greater self-conscious attention to the assumptions that underlie democratic theory *would* channel programmes of research to meet various challenges posed by the theory. Thus far the meandering course of research into mass electoral behaviour has more often followed the decisions of scholars intent on better "understanding" some obvious feature of political topography than testing a normative construction.

W.E. Miller

REFERENCES

1. S. Rice, *Quantitative Methods in Politics,* New York: Knopf, 1928; Jr. S.F. Hayes, "Voter's attitudes towards men and issues", *Journal of Social Psychology*, 2, 1932, pp. 164–82.
2. C.E. Merriam, and H.P. Gosnell, *Non-Voting,* Chicago: University of Chicago Press, 1924.
3. A. Campbell, P.E. Converse, W.E. Miller, and D.E. Stokes, *The American Voter,* New York: Wiley, 1960.
4. J. Prothro, and R. Matthews, *Negroes and the New Southern Politics*, Chapel Hill: University of North Carolina, 1966.
5. A. Campbell, G. Gurin, and W.E. Miller, *The Voter Decides,* Evanston, Ill.: Row Peterson, 1954.
6. A.W. Finifter, "The friendship group as a protective environment for political deviants", *American Political Science Review*, 8, 1974, pp. 607–25.
7. J. Wahlke, H. Eulau, *et al., The Legislative System*, New York: Wiley, 1962.
8. H. Eulau, and K. Prewitt, *Labyrinths of Democracy*, Indianapolis, Ind.: Bobbs-Merrill, 1973.
9. P.F. Lazarsfeld, B.R. Berelson, and W.N. McPhee, *Voting,* Chicago: University of Chicago Press, 1959.
10. W.E. Miller, and J.M. Shanks, *The New American Voter*, Cambridge, Mass.: Harvard University Press, 1996.

Bibliography

Abramowitz, A.J., "Issue evolution reconsidered: racial attitudes and partisanship in the US electorate", *American Journal of Political Science*, 38, 1994, pp. 1–24.

Abramson, P.R., *Political Attitudes in America*, San Francisco: Freeman, 1983.

Aldrich, J.H., "Rational choice and turnout", *American Journal of Political Science*, 37, 1993, pp. 246–78.

Almond, G., and Verba, S., *The Civic Culture*, Princeton N.J.: Princeton University Press, 1963.

Alt, J.E., "The impact of the Voting Rights Act on Black and White voter registration in the South", *Quiet Revolution in the South: The Impact of the Voting Rights Act 1965–1990*, ed. C. Davison and B. Grofman, Princeton, N.J.: Princeton University Press, 1994, pp. 351–77.

Barry, B., *Sociologists, Economists and Democracy*, Rev. edn., Chicago: University of Chicago Press, 1978.

Beck, P.A., "Voters' intermediation environments in the 1988 presidential contest", *Public Opinion Quarterly*, 55, 1991, pp. 371–94.

Berger, B.M., *Working-Class Suburb*, Berkeley: University of California Press, 1960.

Bishop, G., Tuchfarber, J., and Oldendick, R., "The nagging question of question wording", *American Journal of Political Science*, 22, 1978, pp. 250–69.

Bobo, L., "Whites' opposition to busing: symbolic racism or realistic group conflict?", *Journal of Personality and Social Psychology*, 45, 1983, pp. 1196–210.

Borrie, W.D., *The Growth and Control of World Population*, London: Weidenfeld and Nicholson, 1970.

Boudon, R., *Theories of Social Change*, Berkeley: University of California Press, 1986.

Brady, H.E., and Sniderman, P.M., "Attitude attribution: a group basis for political reasoning", *American Political Science Review*, 79, 1985, pp. 1061–78.

—, and Ansolabehere, S., "The nature of utility functions in mass publics", *American Political Science Review*, 83, 1989, pp. 143–164.

Brennan, G., and Lomasky, L., *Democracy and Decision*, Cambridge: Cambridge University Press, 1993.

Burt, R.S., "Social contagion and innovation: cohesion versus structural equivalence", *American Journal of Sociology*, 92, 1987, pp. 1287–35.

Butler, D., and Stokes, D., *Political Change in Britain*, 2nd edn., London: Macmillan, 1969/1974.

Calvert, R.C., "The value of biased information: a rational choice model of political advice", *Journal of Politics*, 4, 1985, pp. 530–55.

Camhis, M., *Planning Theory and Philosophy*, London: Tavistock, 1979.

Campbell, A., Converse, P.E., Miller, W.E., and Stokes, D.E., *The American Voter*, New York: Wiley, 1960.

—, Converse, P.E., Miller, W.E., and Stokes, D.E., *Elections and the Political Order*, New York: Wiley, 1966.

—, Gurin, G., and Miller, W.E., *The Voter Decides,* Evanston, Ill.: Row Peterson, 1954.

Carmines, E.G., and Kuklinski, J.H., "Incentives, opportunities, and the logic of public opinion in American political representation", *Information and Democratic Process*, ed. J.A. Ferejohn and J.H. Kuklinski, Urbana: University of Illinois Press, 1990, pp. 240–68.

—, and McCurley, C., "Mobilization, countermobilization, and the politics of race", *Political Geography*, 14, 1995, pp. 601–19.

—, and Stimson, J.A., *Issue Evolution: Race and the Transformation of American Politics*, Princeton, N.J.: Princeton University Press, 1989.

—, and Stimson, J.A., Huckffldt, R., "Party politics in the wake of the Voting Rights Act", in *Controversies in Minority Voting*, ed. B. Grofman and C. Davidson, Washington, D.C: Brookings Institution, 1992, pp. 117–34.

Chong, D., *Collective Action and the Civil Rights Movement*, Chicago: University of Chicago Press, 1991.

Clifford, P., and Heath, A., "The election campaign", *Heath, Jowell and Curtice 1994*, 1994, pp. 7–24.

Coleman, J.S., *Introduction to Mathematical Sociology*, New York: Free Press, 1964

—, Katz, E., and Menzel, H., *Medical Innovation: A Diffusion Study*, Indianapolis, Ind.: Bobbs-Merrill, 1966.

Converse, P.E., "The nature of belief systems in mass publics", *Ideology and Discontent*, ed. D.E. Apter, New York and London: The Free Press, Collier-Macmillan, 1964, pp. 206–61.

—, "The problem of party distances in models of voting change", *The Electoral Process*, ed. M.K. Jennings, and H. Zeigler, Englewood Cliffs, N.J.: Prentice-Hall, 1966, pp. 175–207.

—, *The Dynamics of Party Support*, Beverly Hills, Calif.: Sage, 1976.

Crewe, I., and Norris, P., "In defence of British election studies", *British Elections and Parties Yearbook 1991*, ed. I. Crewe, P. Norris, D. Denver and D. Broughton. Hemel Hempsted: Harvester-Wheatsheaf, 1992, pp. 3–25.

Dahl, R.A., *Who Governs?*, New Haven, Conn.: Yale University Press, 1961.

Devine, F., "Learning more about political behavior: beyond Dunleavy", *British Elections and Parties Yearbook 1994*, ed. D. Broughton *et al.* London: Frank Cass, 1994, pp. 215–28.

Dewey, J., *Human Nature and Conduct*, New York: Henry Holt, 1922.

Dowding, K., *Political Power and Rational Choice*, Aldershot, Hants.: Edward Elgar, 1991.

Downs, A., *An Economic Theory of Democracy*, New York: Harper and Row, 1957.

Dryzek, J.S., "Australian discourses of democracy", *Australian Journal of Politics*, 29/2, 1994, pp. 221–39.

—, and Berejekian, J., "Reconstructive democratic theory", *American Political Science Review*, 87, 1993, pp. 48–60.

Dunleavy, P., "The growth of sectoral cleavages and the stabilization of state expenditures", *Environment and Planning D: Society and Space*, 4, 1986, pp. 129–44.

—, "Mass political behavior, is there more to learn?", *Political Studies*, 38, 1989, pp. 453–69.

—, *Democracy, Bureaucracy and Public Choice*, Hemel Hemsptead: Harvester-Wheatsheaf, 1991, Chaps. 4 and 5.

—, and Margetts, H., "Auditing democracy: the case for an experiential approach", *Defining and Measuring Democracy*, ed. D. Beetham, London: Sage, 1994, pp. 155–81.

—, and Margetts, H., "The rational basis for belief in the democratic myth", *Preferences, Institutions and Rational Choice*, ed. K. Dowding and D. King, Oxford: Oxford University Press, 1995, pp. 60–88.

Eckstein, G., *Rationale Wahl im Mehrparteiensystem, Die Bedeutung von Koalitionen im räumlichen Modell der Parteienkonkurrenz*, Frankfurt am Main: Peter Lang, 1995.

Eijk, C. Van Der, Niemöller, B., and Tillie, J.N., The two faces of 'future vote': voter utility and party potential, Mimeo.: University of Amsterdam, 1986.

Eldersveld, S.J., *Political Parties*, Skokie, Ill.: Rand McNalley, 1964.

Enelow, J.M., and Hinich, M.J., *The Spatial Theory of Voting*, Cambridge: Cambridge University Press, 1984.

Erbring, L, Goldenberg, E.N., and Miller, A.H., "Front-page news and real-world cues: a new look at agenda setting by the media", *American Journal of Political Science*, 24, 1980, pp. 16–49.

—, and Young, A.A., "Individuals and social structure: contextual effects as endogenous feedback", *Sociological Methods and Research*, 7, 1979, pp. 396–430.

Erikson, R.S., Wright, G.C., and McIver, J.P., *Statehouse Democracy: Public Opinion and Policy in the American States*, New York: Cambridge University Press, 1993.

Esser, H. (ed.), *Alltagshandeln und Verstehen*, Tübingen: Mohr (Siebeck), 1991.

Eulau, H., *Politics, Self, and Society*, New York: Cambridge University Press, 1986.

—, *The Behavioral Persuasion in Politics*, New York: Random House, 1963.

—, and Prewitt, K., *Labyrinths of Democracy*, Indianapolis, Ind.: Bobbs-Merrill, 1973.

Ferejohn, J.A, and Kuklinski, J.H. (eds.), *Information and Democratic Processes*, Urbana: University of Illinois Press, 1990.

Finifter, A.W., "The friendship group as a protective environment for political deviants", *American Political Science Review*, 8, 1974, pp. 607–25.

Fiorina, M., *Retrospective Voting in American National Elections*, New Haven, Conn.: Yale University Press, 1981.

—, "Information and rationality in elections", *Information and Democratic Processes*, ed. J.A. Ferejohn, and J.H. Kuklinski, Urbana: University of Illinois Press, 1990, pp. 329–42.

—, *Retrospective Voting in American National Elections*, New Haven, Conn.: Yale University Press, 1981.

Foucault, M., *Power/Knowledge*, trans. and ed. C. Gordon, New York: Pantheon, 1980.

Fuchs, D., and Klingemann, H.-D., "The left-right scheme: theoretical framework", *Continuities in Political Actions*, ed. M. K. Jennings, J. van Deth *et al.*, Berlin: Walter de Gruyter, 1990, pp. 203–34.

Gans, H.J., *The Levittowners*, New York: Vintage, 1967.

Giles, M.W., and Evans, A., "External threat, perceived threat, and group identity", *Social Science Quarterly*, 66, 1985, pp. 50–66.

Glaser, J.M., "Back to the black belt: racial environment and white racial attitudes in the South", *Journal of Politics*, 56, 1994, pp. 21–41.

Goodin, R.E., and Roberts, K.W.S., "The ethical voter", *American Political Science Review*, 69, 1975, pp. 926–28.

Granovetter, M., "The strength of weak ties", *American Journal of Sociology*, 78, 1973, pp. 1360–80.

Grofman, B., Handley, L., and Glazer, A., "Modeling the link between race and electoral change using aggregate data", Mimeo., University of California, Irvine, 1993.

Guttman, J.M., Hilger, N., and Schachmurove, Y., "Voting as investment vs. voting as consumption: new evidence", *Kyklos*, 47, 1994, pp. 197–207.

Halfpenny, P., *Principles of Method*, London: Longman, 1984.

Hamill, R., Lodge, M., and Blake, F., "The breadth, depth, and utility of class, partisan, and ideological schemata", *American Journal of Political Science*, 29, 1985, pp. 850–70.

Harrop, M., and Miller, W.L., *Elections and Voters*, Basingstoke: Macmillan, 1987.

Hastie, R., "A primer of information-processing theory for the political scientist", *Political Cognition*, ed. R.R. Lau and D.O. Sears, Hillsdale, N.J.: Lawrence Erlbaum Associates, 1986, pp. 11–39.

Hayes, Jr. S.P., "Voter's attitudes towards men and issues", *Journal of Social Psychology*, 2, 1932, pp. 164–82.

Heath, A., and McDonald, S., "The demise of party identification theory?" *Electoral Studies*, 7, 1988, pp. 95–107.

—, Evans, G., Field, J., and Witherspoon, S., *Understanding Political Change: The British Voter, 1964–87*, Oxford: Pergamon, 1991.

—, Jowell, R., and Curtice, J., *How Britain Votes*, Oxford: Pergamon, 1985.

—, Taylor, B. (eds.), *Labour's Last Chance? The 1992 Election and Beyond*, Oxford: Pergamon, 1994.

Himmelweit, H.T., Humphreys, P., Jaeger, M., and Katz, M., *How Voters Decide*, New York: Academic Press, 1985.

Hinich, M.J., and Munger, M.C., "A spatial theory of ideology", *Journal of Theoretical Politics*, 4, 1992, pp. 5–30.

—, *Ideology and the Theory of Political Choice*, Ann Arbor: University of Michigan Press, 1994.

—, and Pollard, W., "A new approach to the spatial theory of electoral competition", *American Journal of Political Science*, 25, 1981, pp. 323–41.

Hoffman, J., *Beyond the State*, Oxford: Polity, 1995.

Hotelling, H., "Stability in competition", *Economic Journal*, 39, 1929, pp. 41–57.

Huckfeldt, R., *Politics in Context: Assimilation and Conflict in Urban Neighborhoods*, New York: Agathon, 1986

—, "Political loyalties and social class ties: the mechanisms of contextual influence", *American Journal of Political Science*, 28, 1984, pp. 399–417.

—, "Social contexts, social networks, and urban neighbourhoods: environmental constraints on friendship choice", *American Journal of Sociology*, 89, 1983, pp. 651–69.

—, and Sprague, J., "Choice, social structure, and political information: the informational coercion of minorities", *American Journal of Political Science*, 32, 1988, pp. 467–82.

—, and Sprague, J., "Citizens, contexts, and politics", in *Political Science: The State of the Discipline II*, ed. A. Finifter, Washington, D.C.: American Political Science Association, 1993, pp. 281–304.

—, "Discussant effects on vote choice: intimacy, structure, and interdependence", *Journal of Politics*, 53, 1991, pp. 122–58.

—, "Networks in context: the social flow of political information", *American Political Science Review*, 93, 1987, pp. 1197–216.

—, "Social order and political chaos: the structural setting of political information", *Information and Democratic Processes*, ed. J.A. Ferejohn and J. H. Kuklinski, Urbana: University of Illinois Press, 1990, pp. 23–58.

—, *Citizens, Politics, and Social Communication*, New York: Cambridge University Press, 1995.

Iversen, T., "The logic of electoral politics: spatial, directional and mobilizational effects", *Comparative Political Studies*, 27, 1994, pp. 155–89.

Iyengar, S., "Shortcuts to political knowledge: the role of selective attention and accessibility", *Information and Democratic Process*, ed. J.A. Ferejohn and J. H. Kuklinski, Urbana: University of Illinois Press, 1990, pp. 281–303.

—, *Is Anyone Responsible? How Television Frames Political Issues*, Chicago: University of Chicago Press, 1991.

—, and Kinder, D.R., *News that Matters*, Chicago: University of Chicago Press, 1987.

Jackman, R.W., "Response to Aldrich's rational choice and turnout: rationality and political participation", *American Journal of Political Science*, 37, 1993, pp. 279–90.

Jennings, M.K., and Niemi, R.G., *Generations and Politics: A Panel Study of Young Adults and Their Parents*, Princeton, N.J.: Princeton University Press, 1981.

—, *The Political Character of Adolescence*, Princeton, N.J.: Princeton University Press, 1974.

Kahnemann, D., and Tversky, A., "Risiko nach Maß-Psychologie der Entscheidungspräferenzen", *Spektrum der Wissenschaft*, 5, 1982, pp. 89–98.

Katz, E., "The two-step flow of political information: an up-to-date report on a hypothesis", *Public Opinion Quarterly*, 21, 1957, pp. 61–78.

Key, Jr. V.O., *The Responsible Electorate: Rationality in Presidential Voting 1936–1960*, New York: Vintage, 1966.

—, and Munger, F., "Social determinism and electoral decision: The case of Indiana", *American Voting Behavior*, ed. E. Burdick and A.J. Brodbeck, Glencoe, Ill.: Free Press, 1959, pp. 281–99.

—, Heard, H., *Southern Politics*, New York, Alfred A. Knopf, 1949.

Klapper, J.T., *The Effects of Mass Communication*, New York: Free Press, 1960.

Klingemann, H.-D., "Measuring ideological conceptualizations", *Political Action*, ed. S.H. Barnes and M. Kaase, Beverly Hills, California: Sage, 1979, pp. 215–54.

—, "Testing the left-right continuum on a sample of German voters", *Comparative Political Studies*, 5, 1972, pp. 93–106

Knoke, D., *Political Networks*, New York: Cambridge University Press, 1990.

Küechler, M., "Issues and voting in the European elections 1989", *European Journal of Political Research*, 19, 1991, pp. 81–103.

Kuklinski, J.H., Luskin, R.C., and Bolland, J., "Where is the schema? going beyond the "s" word in political psychology", *American Political Science Review*, 85, 1991, pp. 1341–55.

Lane, R.E., "Market justice, political justice", *American Political Science Review*, 80, 1986, pp. 383–402.

—, "Procedural goods in a democracy: how one is treated versus what one gets", *Social Justice Research*, 2, 1983, pp. 177–92.

—, *Political Ideology: Why the American Common Man Believes What He Does*, New York Free Press, 1962.

—, *The Market Experience*, Cambridge: Cambridge University Press, 1991.

Langton, K.P., and Rapoport, R., "Social structure, social context, and partisan mobilization: urban workers in Chile", *Comparative Political Studies*, 8, 1975, pp. 318–44.

Laver, M., and Hunt, B.W., *Policy and Party Competition*, London: Routledge, 1992.

Lazarsfeld, P.F., Berelson, B.R., and Gaudet, H., *The People's Choice: How the Voter Makes Up His Mind in a Presidential Campaign*, New York: Columbia University Press, 1948.

—, Berelson, B.R., and McPhee, W.N., *Voting*, Chicago: University of Chicago Press, 1959.

Lijphart, A., *Electoral Systems and Party Systems*, Oxford: Oxford University Press, 1994.

Lindblom, C.E., and Cohen, D., *Useable Knowledge*, New Haven, Conn.: Yale University Press, 1979.

Lindenberg, S., "Rationalität und Kultur, Die verhaltenstheoretische Basis des Einflusses von Kultur auf Transaktionen", *Sozialstruktur und Kultur*, ed. H. Haferkamp, Frankfurt: Suhrkamp 1990, pp. 249–87.

Lodge, M., and Hamill, R., "A partisan schema for political information processing", *American Political Science Review*, 80, 1986, pp. 505–19.

—, McGraw, K.M., Conover, P.J., Feldman, S., and Miller, A.H. "Where is the schema? Critiques", *American Political Science Review*, 85, 1991, pp. 1357–80.

— Hamill, R., McGraw, K.M., and Stroh, P., "An impression-driven model of candidate evaluation", *American Political Science Review*, 83, 1989, pp. 399–419.

Lyotard, J.-F., *The Postmodern Condition*, Minneapolis: University of Minnesota Press, 1984.

MacKuen, M.B., "Social communication and the mass policy agenda", *More than News*, ed. M. MacKuen and S.L. Coombs, Beverly Hills, California: Sage, 1981, pp. 19–146.

—, "Speaking of politics: individual conversational choice, public opinion, and the prospects for deliberative democracy", *Information and Democratic Processes*, ed. J.A. Ferejohn and J. H. Kuklinski, Urbana: University of Illinois Press, 1990, pp. 59–99.

—, Erickson, R., and Stimson, J. Macropartisanship, *American Political Science Review*, 83, 1989, pp. 1125–45.

March, J., *Decisions and Organizations*, Oxford: Blackwell, 1988.

Markus, G.B., and Converse, P.E., "A dynamic simultaneous equation model of electoral choice", *American Political Science Review*, 73, 1979, pp. 1055–70.

Matthews, D.R., and Prothro J.W., "Social and economic factors and negro voter registration in the South", *American Political Science Review*, 57, 1963, pp. 24–44.

McPhee, W.N., Smith, R.B., and Ferguson, J., "A theory of informal social influence", *Formal Theories of Mass Behavior*, ed. W.N. McPhee, New York: Free Press, 1963, pp. 74–103.

Merriam, C.E., and Gosnell, H.F., *Non-Voting*, Chicago: University of Chicago Press, 1924.

Miller, W.E., "One-party politics and the voter", *American Political Science Review*, 50, 1956, pp. 707–25.

—, and Shanks, J.M., *The New American Voter*, Cambridge, Mass.: Harvard University Press, 1996.

Mondak, J.J., "Cognitive heuristics, heuristic processing, and efficiency in political decision making", *Research in Micropolitics*, Vol. IV, ed. M.X. Delli Cappini, L. Huddy, and R.Y. Shapiro, Greenwich, Conn.: JAI Press, 1994, pp. 117–41.

—, "Source cues and policy approval: the cognitive dynamics of public support for the Reagan agenda", *American Journal of Political Science* 37, 1993, pp. 186–212.

Nannestad, P., "Dänisches Wahlverhalten 1971–1979: Ein Modell reaktiven Wählens und einige empirische Ergebnisse", *Parteien, Parlamente und Wahlen in Skandinavien,* ed. F.U. Pappi and H. Schmitt, Frankfurt: Campus, 1994, pp. 285–306.

Nie, N.S., Verba, S., and Petrocik, J., *The Changing American Voter*, Cambridge, Mass: Harvard University Press, 1979.

Oakeshott, M., *Experience and Its Modes,* Cambridge: Cambridge University Press, 1933.

Olson, M., *The Logic of Collective Action*, Cambridge, Mass.: Harvard University Press, 1965.

Ostrom, E., "Metropolitan reform: propositions derived from two traditions", *Social Science Quarterly*, 53, 1972, pp. 474–93.

—, *Governing the Commons*, New York: Cambridge University Press, 1990.

Ottati, V.C., and Wyer, R.S., Jr., "The cognitive mediators of political choice: toward a comprehensive model of political information processing", *Information and Democratic Process,* ed. J.A. Ferejohn and J.H. Kuklinski, Urbana: University of Illinois Press, 1990, pp. 186–216.

Page, B.I., and Jones, B., "Reciprocal effects of policy preferences, party loyalties, and the vote", *American Political Science Review,* 73, 1979, pp. 1071–89.

—, and Schapiro, R.Y., *The Rational Public: Fifty Years of Trends in Americans' Policy Preferences,* Chicago: University of Chicago Press, 1992.

Pappi, F.U., "Die Links-Rechts-Dimension des deutschen Parteiensystems und die Parteipräferenz-Profile der Wählerschaft", *Wahlen und politisches System,* ed. M. Kaase, and H.-D. Klingemann, Opladen: Westdeutscher Verlag, 1983, pp. 422–41.

—, "Parteienwettbewerb im vereinten Deutschland", *Das Superwahljahr, Deutschland vor unkalkulierbaren Regierungsmehrheiten?*, ed. W. Bürklin and D. Roth, Köln: Bund-Verlag, 1994.

Popkin, S.L., *The Reasoning Voter: Communication and Persuasion in Presidential Campaigns*, Chicago: University of Chicago Press, 1991.

Prothro, J., and Matthews, R., *Negroes and the New Southern Politics*, Chapel Hill: University of North Carolina, 1966.

Przeworksi, A., "Contextual models of political behavior", *Political Methodology*, 1, 1974, pp. 27–61.

—, "Marxism and rational choice", *Politics and Society*, 14, 1985, pp. 379–409.

—, and Sprague, J., Paper Stones: A History of Electoral Socialism, *Chicago: University of Chicago Press*, 1986.

Rabinowitz, G., and MacDonald, S.E., "A directional theory of issue voting", *American Political Science Review*, 83, 1989, pp. 93–121.

Rattinger, H., and Krämer, J., "Wahlnorm und Wahlbeleiligung in der Bundesrepublik Deutschland", *Politische Vierteljahresschrift*, 36, 1995, pp. 267–85.

Rice, S., *Quantitative Methods in Politics,* New York: Knopf, 1928.

Rokkan, S., and Lipset, S.M. (eds.), *Party Systems and Voter Alignments*, New York Free Press, 1967.

Ronis, D.L., Yates, J.F., and Kirscht, J.P., "Attitudes, decisions and habits as determinants of repeated behavior", *Attitude Structure and Function*, ed. R.P. Breckler, J. Steven and A.G. Greenwald, Hillsdale, N.J.: Lawrence Erlbaum Associates, 1989, pp. 213–40.

Rose, R., and McAllister, I., *Voters Begin to Choose: From Closed Class to Open Elections in Britain*, London: Sage, 1986.

Rusk, J.G., "Issues and voting", *Research in Micropolitics, ii. Voting Behavior II*, ed. S. Long, Greenwich, Conn.: JAI Press, 1987, pp. 95–141.

Sani, G., "A test of the least distance model of voting choice", Italy, 1972, *Comparative Political Studies*, 7, 1974, pp. 193–208.

Sarlvik, B., and Crewe, I., *Decade of Dealignment,* Cambridge: Cambridge University Press, 1983.

Sartori, G., *Parties and Party Systems*, Cambridge: Cambridge University Press, 1976.

Schumpeter, J., *Capitalism, Socialism and Democracy*, 6th edn. London: Counterpoint; originally published 1943; rpt. 1987.

Sears, D.O., Hensler, C.P., and Speer, L.K., "Whites, opposition to busing, self-interest or symbolic politics?", *American Political Science Review*, 73, 1979, pp. 369–84.

Shively, W.P., "The development of party identification among adults: explorations of a functional model", *American Political Science Review*, 73, 1979, pp. 1039–54.

Simon, H.A., "Human nature in politics: the dialogue of psychology with political science", *American Political Science Review*, 79, 1985, pp. 293–304.

—, *Moods of Man*, New York: Wiley, 1957.

Smith, E.R.A.N., *The Unchanging American Voter*, Berkeley: University of California Press, 1989.

Sniderman, P.M., "The new look in public opinion research", in *Political Science: The State of the Discipline II*, ed. A. Finifter, Washington, D.C: American Political Science Association, 1993, pp. 219–44.

—, Brody, R.A., and Tetlock, P.E., *Reasoning and Choice*, New York: Cambridge University Press, 1991.

—, Glaser, J.M., and Griffin, R., "Information and electoral choice", *Information and Democratic Processes*, ed. J.A. Ferejohn and J.H. Kuklinski, Urbana: University of Illinois Press, 1990, pp. 117–35.

Sprague, J., and Westefield, L.P., "An interpretive reconstruction of some aggregate models of contextual effects", Presented at the annual meeting of the Southern Political Science Association, Gatlinburg, November 1–3, 1979.

Stimson, J.A., *Public Opinion in America: Moods Cycles and Swings*, Boulder, Colo.: Westview Press, 1991.

Sullivan, J.L., Piereson, J., and Marcus, G., "Ideological constraint in the mass public: a methodological critique and some new findings", *American Journal of Political Science*, 22, 1978, pp. 233–49.

Taagepera, R., and Shugart, M.S., *Seats and Votes*, New Haven, Conn.: Yale University Press, 1989, pp. 104–11.

Tedin, K.L., "The influence of parents on the political attitudes of adolescents", *American Political Science Review*, 68, 1974, pp. 579–92.

Tingsten, H., *Political Behavior Studies in Elections Statistics*, Stockholm: Knopf, London: P.S. King, 1937.

Tversky, A., and Kahneman, D., "Judgment under uncertainty, heuristics and biases", *Science*, 185, 1974, pp. 1124–31.

Vanhanen, T., *The Emergence of Democracy: A Comparative Study of 119 States, 1850–1979*, Helsinki: Societas Scientiarum Fennica, 1984.

—, *The Process of Democratization: A Comparative Study of 147 States, 1980–88*, New York: Taylor and Francis, 1990.

Verba, S., and Nie, N.H., *Participation in America*, New York: Harper and Row, 1972.

Wahlke, J., *et al., The Legislative System*, New York: Wiley, 1962.

Weber, M., "On the concept of sociology and the meaning of social conduct", *Basic Concepts in Sociology*, trans. H.P. Secher, New York: Citadel Press; originally published 1925, Ch. 1 of *Wirtschaft und Gesellschaft*, 1966, pp. 29–58.

—, "Social action and its types", *Theories of Society*, ed. T. Parsons, *et al.*, New York: Free Press; one-volume edition, 1965, pp. 173–179.

Wolfinger, R.E., and Arsenau, R.B., "Partisan change in the South, 1952–1976", *Political Parties: Development and Decay*, ed. L. Maisel and J. Cooper, Beverly Hills, California: Sage, 1978, pp. 179–210.

Wright, Jr. G.C., "Community structure and voting in the South", *Public Opinion Quarterly*, 40, 1976, pp. 200–15.

❑❑❑

Index

I

J

K

L

M

N

O

P

V

W

❑❑❑